T0128771

DEDICATION

For Gian Krishna Kaur (Emma) and Devi Parvan
Kaur (Luna). May you always remember that all
things come from God and all things go to God.

THE PATH OF Beauty

A Discovery Of My Sacred Interior

Paula Betancur - Joti Piara Kaur

Order this book online at www.trafford.com
or email orders@trafford.com

Most Trafford titles are also available at major online book retailers.

© Copyright 2019 Paula Betancur - Joti Piara Kaur.
Email: Design@sacredinteriorsbypaula.com
Cover illustration by: Emma Betancur

Print information available on the last page.

ISBN: 978-1-4907-9330-6 (sc)
ISBN: 978-1-4907-9332-0 (hc)
ISBN: 978-1-4907-9331-3 (e)

Library of Congress Control Number: 2019931680

Because of the dynamic nature of the Internet, any web addresses or links contained in
this book may have changed since publication and may no longer be valid. The views
expressed in this work are solely those of the author and do not necessarily reflect the
views of the publisher, and the publisher hereby disclaims any responsibility for them.

Trafford rev. 02/14/2019

 www.trafford.com

North America & international
toll-free: 1 888 232 4444 (USA & Canada)
fax: 812 355 4082

CONTENTS

"Every life is a wonderful story worthy of being told. Every life is a work of art and if it doesn't seem so, perhaps it is only necessary to illuminate the room that contains it.

The secret is to never lose faith, to have confidence in God's plans for us, revealed in the signs with which he shows us the way.

If you learn to listen, you will find that each life speaks to us of LOVE.

Because LOVE is the key to everything, the engine of the world." – Andrea Boccelli.

*"Make yourself so happy, that
when others look at you,
they become happy too."*

– YOGI BHAJAN

INTRODUCTION

The official writing of this book begins on April 20th, 2018. The unofficial writing started many years ago.

After leaving the Delray Beach courtroom and filing for the dissolution of my marriage. Divorce. I finally committed to putting down the words that had been flowing through me for a long time and that if not written and shared, would drown me.

Such words might not be as powerful to you as they are to me, but it is clear that this story must be shared. It might be the most unusual story others have read, or it might just be the most common story. Either way, it is time for me to own it and to share it. This is my story.

Some of it is graphic and clear, some of it might seem vague and conceptual. But it is all real, full of lessons, of emotions and of intuitive messages or revelations that, at times, I have fully acknowledged and followed and other times, -consciously or unconsciously- ignored. Seeing my story down on paper is proof that I am surrounded by such a huge tribe of angels and spirits that have taken care of me and continue to guide me and support me. It is also proof of an ever-flowing love from my Creator. And I believe this is true for you as well.

My purpose with this sharing is to uplift and inspire others through my experiences without attaching any expectation of me changing anyone's world. It is more about me finally understanding and recognizing how resilient we can be, how resilient I have been, as well as embodying and committing to a life that has room for joy and happiness. A happiness that is a choice I have now made, a choice we all can make.

My purpose with this sharing is that others will also be inspired to commit to themselves, love themselves and respect themselves enough to choose to be happy.

Yogi Bhajan says, "Make yourself so happy, that when others look at you, they become happy too." This is precisely my newfound purpose. Who knew, we could be happy after all?

The process of writing this book has been a sort of ritual to me, a rite of passage if you will. It is a symbol of claiming myself. Of unapologetically owning the sides of me that I had not yet owned. Those aspects which my guides and angels keep wanting to bring forth to the light because being truthful and authentic, first and foremost to ourselves, is no longer a choice but a responsibility.

I write this book as I honor my soul and my highest self as well as yours. The spirit child in you and in me that is made of pure love and potential. I write this book to remind myself that I am alive and that it is my birthright and yours to feel happy and reach for the stars that light up and give meaning to the heart. These writings are also a symbol of my gratitude to God and to the Universe, for I finally recognize this earthly life is not meant to be a striving, strenuous struggle, but a true blessing and a unique opportunity.

I refuse to waste any more precious time; not feeling, not laughing, not crying, and not living. SAT NAM.

(*Sat nam* is a Kundalini yoga mantra, and it means: truth is my identity. It is often used as a greeting in the Kundalini yoga community.)

"I am not what happened to me, I am what I choose to become."

-CARL JUNG

CHAPTER 1

My Early Years

I am 32 years old, and I have already lived such a full life. One that I realize hasn't just been full, but has been intricate and heavy to carry. For many years, it has felt like such a burden, yet one that I had no choice but to bear. I know it sounds dramatic and melancholic; perhaps it is to a certain extent due to an accumulation of all the many lives I have already lived. Perhaps it is merely a reality of all the challenges I have encountered in this lifetime. I am an old soul and anyone who has met me can relate to that.

As I dive into all these moments that together have made up my life, I realize each and every situation had a lesson to teach me and something to inspire me to see beyond.

I was born in Colombia and moved to America when I was 13. I had a fairly normal childhood until I was 9, when my dad was killed in Medellin, Colombia due to a drug-related event. After all, it was the 80's in Colombia. A time of drug-related conflict and violence no one could escape. I didn't find out about this part of his death until very recently. I always suspected it, but it was sort of a taboo to be kept and not openly shared.

When I did finally learn the truth, for truth always finds its way to the surface, many pieces of the puzzle of my life came into place. It is as if magic surrounded me when the weight of the secrets of that time was lifted and released. Finding out about this truth, led me to understand a little more about the duality within all of us. The light and the darkness that live inside of each one of us.

It also helped me release a lot of judgement I had carried towards my mother for a long time. It allowed me to see her as a real human being, to understand the weight of her experiences which she has been carrying herself all these years and most importantly, it allowed me to detach my story and who I am now, from who my parents were and who I perceived them to be. Ultimately, learning about my dads death, opened me up to a lot of forgiveness and compassion for both of my parents as well as for myself.

I will never forget the vision I had when the phone first rang to inform my family of his passing. Before hearing anything, I saw the images of his funeral and his casket in my mind. It was such a bizarre feeling and the images so vivid and clear. They weren't quick either. The images lasted in my mind a while, sort of like a movie's trailer.

Our lives were never the same after that as my mother who was only 27 at the time endured one of her greatest challenges. To be a young widow, and the mother of three children, 9 and under. I was the oldest.

For years I watched my mom battle depression, financial difficulties and such an unhappy attitude towards life. We lived with my mom's parents for a few years, moving back and forth as my mom tried to claim her independence. In retrospect and after much healing and letting go of grudges, I recognize she always strived and yearned to be more, and to do more, and was truly dealing with her life in the best and only way she knew at the time.

My mom is now a true testament that love prevails and overcomes anything. While she has endured many more challenges since then, some equally or more difficult, she still has never given up and continues to grow and evolve in her own healing process.

My maternal grandparents were always supportive in the ways they felt they needed to be. I am so grateful for them for doing their best by taking care of us and providing a safe home. I am especially thankful to my grandfather, for he really played such an important role in my life, something I realized not too long ago.

Through his example and very few words, he planted in me seeds of joy and of choosing my thoughts and actions wisely. He is the adult from whom I recall having received the most love and whose presence I felt most strongly during my childhood. His ability to be fully present in the moment was tangible. He would spend endless hours, and sometimes days, working on art projects with me. Drawing perfect shapes of animals, cutting out cardboard, and painting it, seeking supplies… Ah…the memories of looking for sticks and fabric and metal in his old, beautifully organized garage are some of my best!

My grandmother was the boss of the family. She managed the household with order and grace and spent her days cooking, crafting and keeping their accounting. Her joy for handmade home décor surrounded my childhood, and our home was filled with her paintings, pottery, and quilts, among many other of her creative projects. Her joy for art was tangible and she had such a bright light whenever she was in that creative zone. I can still remember her smile and the spark in her eyes during those moments.

I didn't have a lot of contact with my paternal grandparents. I have some memories of our times at their farm, and these few memories are all joyful and full of nature and laughter with cousins, aunts and uncles. It wasn't until I got married that I developed a true curiosity towards the paternal side of my family. It was then when I chose to become more involved and make an effort to get to know them and spend time together. I am grateful for having reconnected with them and learned about their own stories of resilience and of overcoming extremely difficult challenges in their lives.

I am grateful to be able to still have my four grandparents alive and continue to learn from them as I get opportunities to hear more about their journeys.

As my mother battled her depression and worked long hours, never giving up on her obligations and responsibility to provide a good life for her children, I found shelter in books. Especially crafting books and an old English encyclopedia with workbooks and cassettes. I used to play them in a very old cassette player my grandfather lent me. As I now see it, those workbooks became my first altar.

I submerged myself in the world of crafting, making anything, from cutout animals and origami shapes, to painting furniture. I will never forget the first piece of furniture I painted. My own small armoire painted in turquoise with bright pink and blue butterflies and apple green leaves. To this day, these are still my favorite colors.

For several years, I spent my mornings getting dressed in clothes stored in my sweet turquoise butterfly armoire, while listening to Bob Marley's music, which happened to be the first cassette I had with English songs; songs that I would hear on the radio stations and record on my cassette player. There might have been a few Air Supply songs in there as well - a legacy from my mom and dad, who loved Air Supply.

My afternoons would be spent pausing and playing those cassettes as I attempted to write the English lyrics in an effort to learn the songs. After all, there is nothing like being able to sing a song you love! This is where my love for the written word began. There was a certain magic that clicked inside of me when I saw the lyrics of a song. I still feel the same strong connection to the words of any of my favorite songs when I see them and can read them.

Once my hand-crafted art pieces or songs were finished, I would either give them as gifts to friends, or a few beloved teachers, or I would spend another set of endless hours figuring out where to showcase them within the half of the room that I shared with my younger sister. This was a work of art on its own...trying to rearrange my armoire and all these works of art, was not easy with such as small space. This is where my craft project became decorating shoe boxes in which to fit all these treasures. I spent many hours searching for boxes, painting and decorating them - another craft I never even realized I still love - It has always been innate in me to create beauty around me.

As I got a bit older, my crafting decreased and more time was spent with friends. I would try as hard as I could to have sleepovers at other friend's homes. Everywhere else seemed more fun than my own home. The shadows of my dad's death were really beginning to haunt me. There was always so much tension and mystery around adults when the topic of his death was discussed. Not much was said about his death to me, and most of my relatives seemed to focus on how hard the loss was for my mother. The images I created in my mind from overhearing some of the details of his death have haunted me many nights.

I had a great group of girlfriends from school; an all girl's Catholic school. And with time, I started making some friends outside of school. Before I turned 13, and moved to America, I had already had my share of smoking, drinking, exploring several boy crushes and experimenting with pharmaceuticals. Even to the point of attempting suicide by having too many random pills at once. I also secretly "dated" a beautiful green eyed, 27 year old Peruvian tattoo artist during this time.

Having the freedom to engage in these behaviors was very easy. Most of them happened when my mom went away to the US for a few months looking for opportunities for us. She contemplated moving us to another country in search of a better future. It was not too hard to come up with stories for my grandmother to allow me to have sleepovers, and having access to taxis or buses was a piece of cake. So was having access to liquor, cigarettes and even the pharmaceuticals I mentioned earlier which were often simply ordered from the pharmacy and delivered to wherever I was.

I became very good at pretending to be older than I really was, at saying I was somewhere I wasn't and at pretending to be happy when I clearly wasn't. I was "cool" and popular and could get away with so much, making me feel so independent and so in control.

When I moved to America my world was crushed. I left all of my friends behind and had to start over. Thank goodness I had my cousins who have been like siblings to me for so long. They were my friends and my accomplices. We slowly made new friends and learned to have fun in a new way, in a new country, under very different conditions. Much more limiting conditions.

For a few months, I had the "normal" life of a middle school girl. Rode the yellow bus, figured out how to survive socially and whether to go to classes or skip them. Detention...blah, blah, blah. It seemed bland and boring compared to the fun and vibrant life I had in Colombia, full of friends, nature, parties and freedom.

This was until my mother became ill after complications from an ectopic pregnancy from a Puerto Rican guy she had been dating. This part of the story wasn't shared with the rest of my family. I was the first one to find out she was pregnant as I was the one translating for her at the hospital. All those hours spent with my grandfather's encyclopedia learning English came in very handy in order to be able to communicate. I also owe that to my brief student exchange in Kansas City when I was 12 years old which was a good opportunity for me to learn and practice my English. My mom didn't even know of this pregnancy either. We both found out at the same time. It was such a mystery, and there seemed to be so much shame around it.

When she became sick, I took over some of her work. She used to clean houses, so I would often go with her to help. I eventually ended up taking over a few of her clients and worked nights cleaning office buildings and banks. Some of the people she worked for became our biggest angels during such a challenging time. A woman by the name of Sandra who was a hairstylist, even offered to adopt my siblings and me when we found out that Child Protective Services was opening a case on us, as they saw me visit my mom at the hospital, often with no other adult present.

Rolf and Toya, whose house we also cleaned, were our life savers! They took us under their angelic wings and filled our lives with so much generosity and friendship. They often paid for our bills and filled our refrigerator with food. They bought school supplies and clothes for us. They showed my siblings and me so much love and also showed us what having money was truly for. They often took us out to eat or came over to cook for us. They always encouraged us to keep dreaming and to stay positive. They were our angels and I will always hold them so dear to my heart!

My middle school days sucked. I hated every minute of school and cried my eyes out in every class. My only refuge was coloring, drawing and writing letters to all my friends in Colombia.

I often wished I didn't feel so alone and wish I would have been closer to my sister during this time. She was only 3 years younger than me. Instead, I was so angry and resentful of my life that I ended up lashing out at my sister and excluding her. It took me quite a few years to realize how much I hurt her with my actions and my words and I have deeply apologized to her for that.

As I have processed my story during the last few years of my life, one of the saddest reflections I have come across is to realize the lack of empathy and kindness I experienced during my short middle school years. I spent so many hours crying and sleeping in those classrooms, and most of my classmates spent time gossiping about me and speculating on what was possibly wrong with me. I overheard and saw drawings and comments of their speculations: "Is she pregnant? On drugs? Has she been raped?" Yet, not one of those pre-adolescents reached out to lend a hand or show a small act of kindness. There was only one person I remember reaching out to me with deep compassion and a caring heart. It was my social studies teacher, whose name I can't remember, but whose empathy made a difference during my difficult days. I often wish I could find him and thank him for caring, even when it was in the simple form of a kind look, or giving me some extra time to complete assignments.

This makes me sad to think about now, mainly imagining it as the mother that I am now. I would never want my daughters to experience that level of exclusion and of apathy. Middle school was the saddest time of my life until I met my first love: Luis, or Lucho, as many called him.

Because of this time of my life, I hope we are inspired….

* To validate everyone's feelings and experiences, especially Children's, without shaming them or feeling so uncomfortable within us that we want to shut them out.
* To be surrounded by supporting people who empower us and hold us during difficult times. To know when to seek for help and to be grateful for it.
* To give our youth creative outlets and practical tools to channel their feelings. Yoga, breath, music, writing and/or painting.
* To hold tight space for our teens, who easily fool us into being independent and self-sufficient, but who have tender hearts and are so vulnerable.
* To always do what we can to make our children feel safe, loved and know that they belong here with us.
* To empower our loved ones by sharing the truth as a tool to process their past, become more present in the now and feel hopeful for the future.

"You think you are alive because you breathe air? Shame on you. That you are alive in such a limited way. Don't be without love, so you won't feel dead. Die in love and stay alive forever."

RUMI

CHAPTER 2

First True and Eternal Love

I was sitting on my cousin's friend's backyard, hanging out with a bunch of kids I had no interest in but who were my only chance for company. Beer, cigarettes and marijuana all around me. Only one familiar face amid these people, my cousin's -and the great comfort of familiar salsa. Orquesta Narvaez,- reminded me of my friends back at home in Colombia.

I wasn't truly comfortable in this environment, for I didn't know anyone and I could feel the heavy energy. On the outside, it seemed as if I fit in perfectly. Drinking, and smoking and flirting around. I was a mere 14 years old.

Sitting there, I suddenly saw the most beautiful pair of eyes I had ever seen. Deep blue-green, shaped like perfect almonds, above a strong big nose. His chest big and wide, his shoulders strong and young.

He was wearing a white V-neck T-shirt and a sports hat. I looked at him and my heart took a giant leap. I froze for a moment and just could not breathe. He looked at me and smiled with his eyes. His lips did not move at all. I do not know if his heart jumped as mine, but I'd like to think so.

He grabbed a beer and off he went with his friends. Not paying much attention to me. I moved on to my beer, and though I wanted to stare at him, I didn't.

Weeks after that, the same scenario, except now in the backyard of my mom's apartment. The one I shared with my mom, young sister and brother, as well as my grandparents who spent months at a time with us in the US.

Beer and cigarettes purchased for us by my sweet grandfather. Orquesta Narvaez yet again and a more intimate group of people. Four to be exact. Sara, my best friend; Sebas, my cousin; Luis-Blue-Eyed-Perfection, and me. Yes, his name was Luis, and he owned my heart from the moment I saw him. Young and not so innocent, we talked and laughed all night.

As I remember this time of my life, I very well recognize how prematurely I grew up. Still in middle school but working night shifts cleaning local cell phone stores, banks and office buildings and cleaning houses during the weekends. And also drinking and smoking until dawn whenever possible. Not your typical 14-year old, but perhaps more typical than we like to think and accept.

At the end of the night the most beautiful kiss. A kiss that vibrated through my entire body and that I wanted to never end. And this night was the beginning of the non-traditional, young romantic story of the first love of my life.

For the next few years, we spent every possible minute together.

Sometimes this meant stealing my mother's car in the middle of the night without even having a driver's license. I would drive to his house in Weston, 30 minutes away from where I lived. We would spend the night making love and watching TV, sometimes smoking pot and then making love once again.

Our lovemaking nights were full of magic. My young body full of juices for him, we enjoyed the delicious pleasure of being together, escaping the noisy chaos of my mind. Tears often rolling down our cheeks as we connected in a way we couldn't quite feel thankful for yet. Not consciously at least. We were so little! But we were addicted to each other. Time froze when we were together and having to go back home to my reality was the worst part of the time I spent with him.

Little did we know how divine this love was. Little did we know at this young, immature stage of our lives, that this would be a story to write about one day. Little did I know, that I would spend over a decade dreaming of him, connected to him, even after he transcended into the spirit world.

In my world of responsibility with school, siblings, work and a sick mother, Luis was my refuge. My chance at friendship, companionship, joy, life and hope. His life seemed more normal than mine, way more normal. His mom was a single mother of three boys. He was the oldest -as I was- and his only responsibility was school. During our years together, he occasionally held a job just to get money for us, for going out or shopping for cool brand-name clothes.

My cleaning job, however, was an essential source of income at home. I never questioned that, though at times I felt overwhelmed. Quitting was not an option. Lucho, as we called him, would spend his nights cleaning with me, so that I could get out of those buildings faster and spend more time with him.

We made love in every office I ever cleaned, and in every parking lot where we parked. Life without him simply would have had no meaning or joy.

The four years we spent together were full of fun, lovemaking, dancing, singing, movies, motorcycle rides, fights, cheap hotels, occasionally a fancy one, driving without a driver's license, poetry, letters, gifts, flowers, chocolate, alcohol, pot, laughter, tears, work, fear, pain, disapproval and love.

Lucho was a sweet, gentle soul. Introverted and shy, yet strong and adventurous. He loved me deeply and took care of me. He helped me with money when I needed and always offered a hug and a kiss when I fell apart. Lucho had his own longing to belong. His emptiness came from the lack of a father figure in his life. He craved that male connection so much and had grand plans to become successful so his dad could feel proud of him. That was one of his biggest dreams.

One day, he gave me the most precious gift, one I had always wanted: a short-haired beige Chihuahua; Nemo, which became my baby.

Luis always supported my dreams, even when others didn't. He also became my most faithful model as I went into cosmetology school. I tried every haircut, manicure, pedicure and even make up on him. He was my best friend, my accomplice and my lover. He made my life worth living, and I never cried again at school after he came into my life. I had suddenly found a reason to live.

A few months after Nemo came into my life, I had a disturbing dream. It's hard to remember all of it, but it was a dream of hardship and loss. Lucho's red motorcycle was there, and he was in some sort of institution and I vividly remember standing by the doors of this place without being able to find him inside. There was an intense feeling of knowing something terribly bad had happened to Luis and I kept seeing him far away from me, even though we were physically in the same area. I woke up distressed with a sense of loss and called him to share. He asked me not to think about it and to not talk about it anymore because it scared him. He loved his motorcycle so much, but there was always that sense of danger around it.

I unwillingly let go of the dream that chased me, until about a week later, on December 24th. We spent the day together and planned on spending Christmas Eve with my family. He would sleep over as he often did, and we would be together on Christmas morning. He would then leave to be with his family for the rest of the day.

This kind of arrangement was normal for us for the last few years. We tried to share as much time as we could, and our mothers often disliked it. We were so young after all. But no amount of nagging or trying to enforce curfews could keep us away from each other. That day his mom called and asked him not to stay with me the night but to spend it with her instead, for one reason or another. Now I know it was his mother's intuition speaking.

He felt guilty somehow and told me that he would please her. I wasn't too happy about it, but I was never pleased when we had to part ways. I hated saying goodbye to him, even if it was just for a day or two.

I walked him down to the parking lot, and we sat inside my red Beetle. We kissed goodbye, and the kiss became the most beautiful lovemaking. After all, parking lots and cars were our staples. We said how much we loved each other. He would come over the next day for lunch, and we would spend Christmas afternoon together.

He left, and this was the last time I ever saw him in physical form.

That night, after spending Christmas Eve with his mom and family, he went to a party with some friends. He had recently moved further away to Miami and had a new set of friends. Strangely, I did not like them much, even though if I had never met them. He never told me about this party. In fact, he called me when he got home after being with his family to say goodnight. This was the last time I heard his voice.

On Christmas day, 2004 at 11.29 a.m., I received a voicemail from his friend, saying Lucho had been in an accident. I immediately remembered what I dreamt a few days before and just knew this was not a simple accident. I could not get a hold of his family or anyone who knew him. I called hospitals and police stations, but nobody knew anything about him. Finally, a nurse from Jackson Memorial told me there was someone with the same last name in that hospital and I found out it was his brother. I didn't understand why Lucho wasn't in the same hospital. I begged her to please ask his mother to call me if she was there. Three hours later I finally get a call from his mom.

"Lucho is dead Paulita," she said, "He is dead."

My entire world stopped and crumbled. My mind could not process this. My vision blurred, and my heart stopped. I could not hear or see. I felt as if I could not breathe. The pain in my heart was unbearable. I felt as if my heart was ripped out of my body. As if I was utterly incomplete. Unable to keep going. I was sure my life was over. This feeling of powerlessness and devastation was a part of my world for many months. From that day on and for the next year or so, I spent my life crying with my dog, pretending to move on, and then crying some more. I spent a lot of time with his mother, and we brought so much comfort to each other. Every night I slept with his T-shirt on, the V-neck he was wearing when we first met. I missed him. I never knew a person's heart could break in so many pieces and was still be able to maintain life. My life! I did not want it! How could I die and meet him where he was? That is all I wanted to do. Die.

Miraculously, I did not die. Somehow, and by the grace of God, without any real tools to manage my pain, but with a couple of amazing friends, I kept going, as well as I could manage.

I remember my dear friend Veronica trying to cheer me up and taking me out, only to find me hiding and crying in every corner of every party. She was with me during the most challenging moments of this pain, and I will forever remember that. She always had tears of her own to share with me and ears that would listen for hours and hours.

That same December, I graduated from cosmetology school. My graduation was December 27th, but I didn't go. It was a big accomplishment but not as big as the pain I was in. I did a little bit of traveling The next May and went to visit my cousin in Canada. I spent 10 days crying in Canada. Wherever I went, I would cry. I poured my heart and soul into every tear I cried. I received so much love and compassion from my cousin and his girlfriend who welcomed me in their apartment and did everything they could to comfort me.

This was definitely the time where my spiritual journey began. After Lucho's death. This is the time where I felt I couldn't go on unless a higher power had guidance for me. I looked and longed for more.

I desperately needed my life to have meaning and to understand why this pain and hardship could be a part of such a short life. I knew there had to be a bigger plan for me because I was able not only to cope with this kind of stuff at my age but to help others as well. I often heard what a comfort it was for others to be around me, how inspired they felt by how I was handling my life and my love for my family and Luis. I didn't get it. I was just doing what I had to do.

It often simply came in the way of being fully present with my feelings. Not because I was mindfully trying to do so, but because the feelings where bigger than me and overtook me like a giant wave. Even if I wanted to try to shut the tears off, their power was greater than me. I went to bereavement support groups and became great friends with senior widows. Women and men in their late seventies and eighties. I was 18. How could these seniors and a young adult be going through the same loss? The loss of a loved one. This never crossed my mind. I never saw any of these people as "old". I saw them as people who also understood the deep pain of death and who were there for me through my tears, and I was there for them. I visited every church I encountered and every bereavement support group I could find. I went to Catholic churches, Christian churches, Baptist churches, and a few others in between.

These sacred places were my refuge. Silence was my shelter. The faith of the people around me was my hope. Their devotional music allowed me to feel and uplifted me. It was not about religion for me at all. In fact, I think I never really labeled each of these churches I visited as religious places. I just felt supported by the energy and the kindness of strangers who cared about my story. Sometimes silently showing me they cared.

Slowly, after about a year, I felt a little bit more human again. Working at a well-known spa, building my clientele doing hair. My mother had finally recovered and was working again, so I was no longer a main financial provider at home. All of this gave me a chance to stand up again and breathe new air.

I met many wonderful women at my new job. Women who became my friends and practically family. Without their support, their prayers, their listening ears, I would have never been able to get through my pain.

Because of this time of my life, I hope we are inspired....

* To allow ourselves to experience the magic of someone's soul shining through their eyes.
* To feel with an open heart the power of love. The kind of love that covers you with goosebumps and tingling warmth through your entire body.
* To allow the heart to feel completely broken when we lose someone we love that much.
* To recognize and offer empathy to anyone who is also feeling and experiencing the pain of loss.
* To experience the joy and unconditional love of pets and animals.
* To value the power of friendship and love, for they are the colors of our lives.

"We don't meet people by accident, they are meant to cross our path for a reason"

- RUBYAANNE

CHAPTER 3

A Coffee and a Safer Refuge

It was a Monday, my day off from the spa. I took my mom to the dentist. She needed to get her wisdom teeth out. I was not very interested in going with her, but I drove her to his office 30 minutes away from our home. She went in for her appointment, and as soon as she did, I leaned over the front desk to ask where I could get a coffee nearby.

A smiling and welcoming man wearing blue scrubs answered. "Oh, I can make you some coffee in the back. Come on in." *Oh, well that's nice,* I thought, *though I was hoping to sit at a nice coffee shop and not at a dentist office, but ok...*" So I went in. In a small kitchenette in the back of the office, he poured me a cup of coffee. It was good Colombian coffee. We chatted for a few minutes and were interrupted by a young woman. "Doctor, your patient is ready and waiting for you."

"Excuse me," he said. "I need to go to do a wisdom teeth surgery."

"Oh! You are the doctor?" I said. "Well, what have you been doing here making me coffee? I thought you were an assistant or something. That's my mom in there!" He laughed and went on his way.

A few minutes later my mom's procedure was finished, and she was ready to go. Her dentist and my coffee maker walked her out to the lobby. After giving her a few final recommendations, he turned to me and asked me if there was a chance I wanted to model for his health magazine. I declined politely and let him know I did not like having my picture taken and was not a model. He said something in a funny tone to my mom, along the lines of "have a good day, mother in law."

"Actually, my mom is the one interested in a boyfriend. Not me" I said, smiling sarcastically. I thought he would be a great match for my mom. I couldn't quite figure out how old he was, but he seemed old enough to date my mom, was also Colombian and was a doctor! What a great catch for her!

The next day my mom got a personal call from him wanting to know how she was doing. *Wow, quality service!* I thought. I never heard of a doctor in this country personally calling a patient just to check on them. Then my mom gave me the phone, "It's doctor Betancur..." she said. "He wants to talk to you."

"What? Me? Why?" I scoffed.

When I grabbed the phone, he asked me how I was and reiterated his interest in having me take pictures for his magazine. "No, thank you" I said again, "I am just not interested." He told me to give him a call if I changed my mind and I thanked him. *Weird*, I thought.

A couple of weeks went by, and on a Friday afternoon, as I was ready to leave the spa for the day, I checked my schedule and realized someone had booked a man's haircut at 7 p.m. It was 5 p.m. Now I had to wait for a guy for two hours. For a simple haircut. Men's hairstyles, as my former colleagues will tell you, were not my strength or joy.

I waited and when 7 p.m. came, he showed up. I was so surprised to see it was my mom's dentist. I cut his hair, a simple short haircut, thank God. We chatted a little, and as I finished, he asked me out. "Do you have any plans for tonight? Let's go have dinner, it's Friday night", he said.

"No, thank you," I replied.

"Oh, come on," he said. "Just dinner, I have to eat nearby since I drove over an hour to get my haircut here, and surely you could use a drink and some food after a long day of work."

"I'm not interested, really. Thank you."

He accepted my response, gave me a $100 bill as a tip, a kiss on the cheek and I didn't see him again for a few months. He continued to check on my mom often asking about me, I suspected.

One day, just after Hurricane Wilma hit Florida, I was sitting in the apartment where I lived with my mom and siblings. My grandparents who were now based in Colombia but were visiting at the time, were there as well. I heard a knock on the door. At that time, we were out of power, with little food (and certainly, no hot food). Our sliding glass balcony door was broken, and there was a massive tree on top of my mom's car. Not a very fun time.

When I opened the door, there he was, with bags of water and warm food and pastries as well as with gas and a generator! *An angel*, we all thought.

After some time with us in the apartment, taking care of my grandparents and winning them over with his latin jokes and fiery energy, he asked if I wanted to have dinner soon. How could I resist? He had just freaking saved my family! Well, not exactly, but it sure felt like it.

He invited me to dinner at his house that week. When I walked in, we had a glass of white wine, and we chatted for a bit. He led me to his backyard where his small boat was anchored on the canal leading to the Intracoastal. We were taking the boat to a well-known restaurant nearby, Bush's. We had a wonderful dinner and spent the night talking about food and laughing at his jokes.

On the way back to his house, he anchored the boat for a few minutes to enjoy Florida's cool October breeze (a rare occurrence). We chatted some more, and he proceeded to kiss me. It was such a magical night, with trees all around the water, and stars in the sky, with beautiful, luxurious boats passing by. We spent the whole night chatting at his house and smoking cigarettes and drinking more wine. He made me laugh like no one ever had!

By the end of the night, I had had way too much wine, but I was determined to go home. In my attempt to get up, I got so sick, I threw up everywhere. He cleaned me up and took me to his bed to sleep. I passed out for a couple of hours and woke up, still drunk, determined to leave. I did. After all, I was used to drunk driving from my years of sneaking out at night to see Lucho.

Loveland

A few days after, most people were still out of work due to the damage from the storm. The spa was closed until further notice and so was Alvaro's practice. He invited my family and me to his house.

We showed up and he cooked for us. He made fish and steamed vegetables. The fish was so delicious. It was the first time I ever had good fish. Little did I know there was such a thing. Good fish!

During dinner, he surprised me with an envelope. He knew we would be out of work for a few more days and thought it would be fun to go skiing in Colorado. He had already bought the tickets and asked me if I wanted to come.

Colorado? I barely know this man. *How can I just go on a trip with him? Then again…it does sound like fun!* I said yes. My family didn't seem too surprised. They really liked him. I could tell.

A few days later, we sat at the airport waiting to board, and still did not know exactly where we were going to ski or stay. We were flying to Denver, but that was as much as we knew. As we Googled away with our phones, he found a small town, just 45 minutes away from Denver, where the slopes were already open. It was early October. The name of the town: Loveland. How perfect.

Loveland was magical. We stayed in a cozy and old log cabin. We skied and skied and we enjoyed delicious tomato basil soup and white wine at night. We talked and laughed and hugged and kissed. When it came time to make love, which of course was inevitable, I could only go so far.

After my top came off, I could not help but experience a flood of tears overwhelming my heart and pouring down my face… The memories of my sweet lovemaking with Lucho would come up and consume my thoughts and heart. I could not dare to make love to anyone else. Not yet at least.

Alvaro was awfully patient and respectful. He held me for many nights in his arms, not pushing me any further. He held space for my tears and understandingly let me know he would wait until I was ready.

I was so grateful for his embrace and his warmth. We managed to have a great time during our trip without further intimacy. He kept telling me he knew I was the one for him and he would wait as long as needed. I felt so hopeful and so secure.

After we came back home, it was unofficially official. We were dating and everyone knew. We went out for dinners, had way too much wine, danced and had fun with friends occasionally and he would always strive to include my grandparents, mom and siblings.

Our first intimate time together was beautiful. Feeling stronger and more comfortable with him, I allowed my body to guide me. We were at his home, having wine on the boat. The night was clear, and the stars were out. We fooled around in the boat's cabin and I knew this was happening. I remember his loving way and how fully in the moment I felt.

From this moment on, we spent every weekend together. We traveled some, skied a lot, and really enjoyed our time together. Everyone around me was grateful for him. After all, he helped me smile again and experience life in a way that was new to me. He was a great friend, kind, generous, fun. He shared my culture, had a fantastic career, and really knew how to have a good time.

Our time together was full of abundance and laughter. It all felt easy and comfortable.

About seven months later, on June 4th - the anniversary of my dad's death - he proposed. After having talked for hours that night about how it would look like if we got married and how sure he was that I was the one, he asked me if I would marry him. I immediately said yes. Of course, I would marry him. He was the best person in the world for me, and I was sure there was no one else like him. A man that cared about me this much certainly was meant to be my husband.

He gave me a gold diamond ring. Sized too big. I didn't wear it right away. Not only because it didn't fit, but also because we wanted to make it formal and for him to ask for my hand in front of my family. He did and it was so sweet and beautiful.

Because of this time of my life, I hope we are inspired….

* To be grateful for the generosity of other people's actions.
* To be willing to take risks, to laugh uncontrollably and to be adventurous.
* To be truthful to our bodies when they speak to us.
* To honor people's journeys and allow them to go at their own rhythm.
* To allow love to take down the high walls of a broken heart.

"Love bears all things, believes all things, hopes all things, and endures all things. Love never fails."

– 1 CORINTHIANS 13:7

CHAPTER 4

The Beginning of Marriage

We got married in August 2006. That same year my mom was diagnosed with breast cancer. Alvaro was my biggest support during that time of fear. So many flashbacks of all the previous difficulties we had endured as a family with a sick mom haunted me. But this time I knew my brother, sister and I had more support. I felt so safe having my husband's support.

Our wedding at the Boca Raton Country Club was beautiful. My mom, a former wedding planner who was going through chemotherapy and radiation, had the time of her life planning the wedding with me. We had close to 200 guests and an amazing live band who sang a diverse repertoire in Spanish and English. Drinks and delicious food and gorgeous flower centerpieces made by my mother. In retrospect, I realize I had that wedding more for her than for myself.

My new husband and I danced through the night and sang away with the surprise mariachi band he brought for me. I barely sat and didn't even eat the delicious lobster ravioli I had so carefully selected for the menu. We were so happy on our wedding day.

Alvaro and I had talked about wanting to start a family right away and were openly welcoming the possibility of becoming pregnant at any time. I always made sure he was aware that my "parenting" responsibility came first with my little brother, who was 13 at the time. He always agreed and was supportive of my caretaking of Santiago. I made him promise that if I ever needed to legally adopt Santy or have him move in with us, he would be okay with that. He promised, willingly. I was also very clear that I was not interested in having kids unless I could stay home with them and raise them myself. He absolutely agreed.

We began trying to conceive. Months and months went by. After what felt like an eternity but was only a year and a half, I peed on a stick, which told me I was pregnant.

My first gut feeling as I was in that bathroom alone was fear. I was so afraid and almost immediately saw a vision of blood in my head. It lasted a microsecond, and after sitting in that toilet for a moment, staring at the images speeding in my head, and numb within, I got up to share the news with my husband.

He was thrilled. Thrilled. A dream come true. I smiled. With a yearning for joy but with an inner knowing that I could not express but my soul recognized. Grief.

I proceeded to book my Ob-gyn appointment a few days later. And that's when the excitement took over! A heartbeat! Oh! The sound of that heartbeat and how it transforms you. At that moment, I experienced the miracle of the divine power in its magnitude. I was blown away by that galloping sound. Absolutely blown away.

I didn't yet recognize these feelings of miracles and divinity in my exterior or in my life at the time. I couldn't verbalize or express it, but I now believe all women who experience listening to that heartbeat are transported there. To a space of wholeness and divine power. A connection to source. It's a feeling full of ether. Not yet tangible but coming through as the vibration and sound of a beating heart.

Of course, we told all our friends and family. Such excitement and love for the baby on the way! I was grateful and all feelings of fear just slipped away. I had never dreamt of this new life. It was amazing.

I was excited and eager to experience this new journey and I started journaling all my feelings and the dreams I had for this baby. I collected all that I wanted to learn and live with him in a scrapbook. It was a beautiful time of my life, to feel joy and excitement for something so beautiful. I wasn't used to that. It was actually not comfortable to feel so excited. It felt strange and foreign, yet I was doing my best to embrace it.

Because of this time of my life, I hope we are inspired....

* To experience each moment with fun and with joy.
* To dance to loud music and let go of the seriousness of life.
* To see the big miracles that the smallest things really are.
* To be willing to allow our excitement for life, to be expressed and shared.

"I'll see you in my dreams tonight.
I'll kiss your cheek and hold you
tight. I have no tears left to cry.
You've flown away my butterfly..."

– Angela Schneider

CHAPTER 5

Too Good to be True

My miscarriage took place on December 8th, 2008. I will never forget that day and have secretly honored it every year since then.

I was in NYC at the time, accompanying my husband to a dental convention. I was 10 weeks pregnant and spent my day hanging out with my old friend, Andres, who had become a great companion when Luis passed away, and before meeting Alvaro.

All that day I felt a bit crampy but didn't pay much attention to the signals my body was giving me, until around 3 p.m. when I saw some bright red spotting in my underwear.

I was sad. Not afraid. I just needed to rest. I had a bit of spotting a few weeks before, but my doctor said it was probably implantation bleeding as it was early on. I went to the hotel where I was staying, met my husband in our room, and I just laid down to take a nap.

We had planned for a nice dinner, but I really didn't feel like going out. I wanted silence and solitude, though nothing seemed to be happening.

A few hours later I went to the bathroom, and this is where it started. Blood clots coming out of me. Dripping so heavily and thick. I saw the blood, just like in my vision the day I took that pregnancy test and just like in some dreams I had, but I thought every woman had them at the beginning of pregnancy.

I saw that blood in real life. I yelled for my husband who immediately came into the bathroom. He wanted to go to the hospital. I responded I didn't want to go to the ER on a Friday night in Manhattan. I knew it would be stressful and crowded and I needed solitude, and I was going to be ok. There was nothing to be done. I could feel it for sure.

I looked at Alvaro, and I said: "No. We are losing this baby right now and I just want you to be here with me." And so, he stayed and sat on the edge of the luxurious hotel bathroom and held my hand while I bled and bled and bled for hours. I cried my eyes out in silence with the most profound devotion to my mourning. To the death of my dreams. Our dreams of a family. I just cried in denial but at the same time, with a profound knowledge of what was happening. I stopped bleeding and decided to stand up and go to bed. As I sat down I called my mom, crying quietly, and I told her I had just lost the baby. I had lost him.

I still often think of my baby boy. And no, the gender was never revealed to me, but I just knew. I knew it was my boy. Maximiliano. Ever since then I have dreamt of him many times. I still do. I still feel him.

Moving On

Telling everyone about the loss was just like my previous experiences with death. There were the same feelings of sadness and grief as when my father and boyfriend passed away. But to the world, the miscarriage was just a statistic. At least it felt that way. "One out of four women experience miscarriages". I felt so alone. So alone.

I couldn't share my feelings with anyone because I didn't know they were real. They were real inside me, of course, but who could understand? How could I even verbalize them without breaking down? Any time I tried, I faced comments such as: "It wasn't meant to be," "it wasn't a real baby yet" or "you can always try again, you are so young."

I shared some of my sadness with my husband, and he always had a hug to offer. But making sense of my experience wasn't yet a part of my being. It was such an automatic thing for me to just know what had happened but also to feel numb right after.

For months I felt so sad and so frozen. It was like life was proving to me that the feeling of safety and happiness I experienced after meeting Alvaro and getting married couldn't last too long. *Too good to be true,* that was my inner mantra. Struggle, death, hardship: that felt natural and normal to me. Happiness and joy? Nah! That only lasts a little bit.

Because of this time of my life, I hope we are inspired….

* To genuinely support women that go through miscarriage and pregnancy loss and to validate their experiences.
* To be ok with feeling afraid and sad.
* To learn how to speak to a woman going through these losses by saying things like: "I'm sorry this happened" or "I know how much this meant to you, you must really be hurting right now."

"I surrender to the power of nature as I celebrate a new cycle of birth within myself"

– ANONYMOUS

CHAPTER 6

Connecting to the Bigger Picture

I now realize, that my miscarriage was such a pivotal moment in my life. I finally learned to trust my intuition a little more. Gut feelings, dreams, visions…they matter. I learned to accept that I couldn't always plan my life and expect it to be perfectly smooth and effortless now that I felt safe and secure with my husband.

During this time, I experienced anger towards my past and my upbringing. I experienced so much chaos and stirring inside. I was angry at the unfairness of life. I desperately needed to make sense of so much, instead of just riding along with whatever life brought me. I recognized I couldn't plan my life on a spur-of-the-moment practice. If I wanted a plan, it had to be aligned with a higher perspective. A bigger vision.

Now, it is important to clarify that at that time I could not adequately express that recognition. It was more a feeling than a clear message.

I decided this was the time I was going to focus on pursuing my Interior Design degree. I continued working as a stylist for a bit longer while I went to school. Eventually, as I felt more and more passionate about my Interior design school, and with my husband's support, I decided to go to school full time and quit working at the spa.

It was during this period that I learned how to meditate through the practice of Transcendental Stress Management. A gift from my husband. One of his patients, Mike, discussed bartering this meditation course for a dental procedure. I encouraged them however to keep the energy of the dental treatment and the meditation course separate by not bartering but paying each other instead. It felt as if these energies didn't need to be mixed and I felt that paying for the class would increase our level of commitment as my husband and I embarked into the world of meditation. This practice became a beloved tool to me and took me a step further into taking control of my physical body and my mind. It also opened many doors to a more holistic lifestyle. I began juicing every day and eating cleaner. It made an incredible difference in my life.

After a few months, I was able to understand that I wasn't quite ready to be a mom at that exact moment and that I wanted to spend more time getting to know my husband and discussing what our parenting would be like. I chose to engage in "my plan" in a more active way and at the same time to trust that if it was for my highest good to conceive a child, then God would certainly present that to me. It was not always easy to achieve a balance; the art of knowing when to control and when to let go after all, is one that we can spend many lifetimes learning about. But at least I tried and let go more than ever before.

The journey of conception can be tough for many women. It certainly was for me. And because of my experience, I tapped into a different level of compassion towards other women who might have been going through the same experience. The experience of miscarriage also opened my heart to a different way of experiencing death and loss and years later brought the need to talk openly about it with more people. I wasn't ready to be a mom yet because there still was so much I needed to learn, so much I needed to heal, and because the true intention of why I wanted to be a mom was not yet fully grasped. Having a child was something I wanted but, where did that yearning come from?

I began exploring and studying the topics of vaccination, gentle discipline, natural pregnancy, and birth. This brought my husband and I closer than ever and connected us to our vision of becoming parents with so much love to give. It also brought a bigger understanding of the soul of a child coming through for her own journey and the lessons to be learned and taught on the earth. It is a bigger responsibility to be a part of that, than just raising a child to be an extension of us as parents.

After three years of marriage, we conceived again. This time it was pure joy from the beginning. I was truly excited to meet my Emma. That's the name of our firstborn. She was named after Alvaro's deceased adopted sister, whom he adored! Her name means universal and whole and her middle name, Nicollette, means victory.

Our pregnancy with Emma was magical. In the beginning, as I received prenatal care from an Ob-gyn, there was still that feeling of fear as medical tests and hormonal results didn't look too promising to my doctor. It wasn't until I decided not to live in fear of expecting to bleed my baby out at every moment, that the magic started. I decided to switch doctors and to fully listen and trust my body this time, instead of relying on a number in a piece of paper, to tell me whether I could have my baby or not.

My pregnancy was perfect. My diet was perfect. I did prenatal yoga almost daily. I journaled. I designed the perfect Serena and Lily organic nursery. It was pure happiness and bliss.

I never felt more beautiful, bountiful, and happier! I felt I was truly a goddess. The experience of conscious pregnancy absolutely changed me. I learned to go within so much deeper than ever. I learned to connect with the soul of my baby, with the unborn parts of me, with the scared parts of me. I learned to take care of myself and create a peaceful environment for myself and my family.

This is also the time when I first came upon Kundalini yoga. I learned that my baby was learning from my own state of consciousness while she was in the womb and that my experiences would become the foundation of her subconscious. This was extremely powerful and allowed me to be so in tune with the miracle of life. It also encouraged me to take full charge and responsibility of my body, my baby and my birth.

Because of this time of my life, I hope we are inspired....

* To trust that the Universe always takes care of all our needs.
* To rely on our own intuition and take the necessary steps to develop it further.
* To love our bodies in every stage of our life.
* To create environments that nourish our loved ones and us.

"The purest thing in the world is the heart of a mother, the heart chakra, the center of the mother. It can move God. It can move the Universe. It can cause an effect beyond limitation. The heart of the mother is the greatest power of infinity ever given to any finite being."

– Yogi Bhajan

CHAPTER 7

Emma's Birth Story

E mma, was born on December 16th, 2009.

At around midnight I started noticing contractions strong enough that they didn't let me sleep. I had been feeling a little crampy during the day, but nothing more. It was a long day and I went to bed at around 11 p.m. When I finally got up and couldn't sleep anymore, I wondered if this was it. If it was time for her to be born.

I turned on my iPod and got on all fours doing some Cat and Cow poses, as I practiced some visualizations and hypnobirthing affirmations. I kept waiting for a sign that said: "This is it. My baby is coming."

I moved around the room and would lie down on my side whenever I could to try to get some sleep, though that wasn't possible. Alvaro slept soundly and had no clue I was up. Around 3 a.m. I started timing my surges as they came faster and stronger. I went to the bathroom, and there it was. My sign. A bloody show. I knew my baby girl was on her way!

I changed my clothes into my "labor outfit" and put on the angel pin that I received at my blessing way and lit my blessing way candle. Finally, I awoke Alvaro. "Baby...it's time. The baby is coming."

Alvaro got up and started doing his "job": making sure the pillows and bags were ready to go. As each contraction came stronger and stronger, I went deeper into myself and my music. To this day, I use birthing as a reference to the power of going within.

I remembered my deep breathing techniques and felt comfortable while laboring on my hands and knees or sitting with my head forward on an ottoman.

We decided to call Mindy, our doula, around 4.30 a.m. She arrived shortly after and my contractions kept getting stronger and stronger. I got in the tub. *Ahhh!* That felt so good. I was talking between contractions and remember thinking: *Hmmm this isn't too bad... A bit challenging but I can totally do it.*

I had some food and juice while in the tub. I wasn't too hungry but wanted some food on me since I knew I would not be able to eat at the hospital.

Finally, we called our midwife and decided to go to the hospital at 6:30 a.m. Alvaro also called my mom to meet us there. Shortly after our arrival, I was checked by my midwife. "You are 4-5 centimeters," she said.

Ok, I'm five. This should be quick, I thought.

Contractions escalated, and I found myself moaning and making noises. I was sitting on the bed or the birthing ball most of the time and remember circling my body very subtly. I still don't know if I was moving more in my mind than I was physically. I would open my eyes between contractions, but otherwise, they were closed most of the time. A true journey within.

The temperature changes of my body where crazy! I felt burning hot during my contractions, and wow! The cold wet towels my Midwife put on my neck and forehead felt like heaven. Then I would be freezing cold right after the surges. I was shivering. It was difficult to adjust.

My music was amazing. I couldn't have done it without it. As I was at a point where I thought the pain and the intensity was the maximum I could stand, I got in the shower with Alvaro by my side. I'm pretty sure this was the most spiritual part of my birth and the moment I wanted to escape it the least. I felt so out of my body and in another realm during this moment and the water and Alvaro's sweet strokes felt terrific.

I felt so raw and as if I had completely lost control and surrendered. I remember crawling on the bathroom floor to get in the shower and Mindy getting me up saying: "you don't really want to be on "that" floor".

What I remember the most from this moment in the shower is my husband's kisses and him caressing my head in a way I had never felt before. His hands and eyes were so full of love and admiration for me. I felt so blessed. I also remember a powerful urge to push. I really thought my baby was ready to come out right there.

I got out of the shower and just completely lost it, in a way where I just couldn't do it any longer. I felt such pressure and so much doubt and was just overwhelmed. I felt thirsty and hungry and exhausted. Terry, my midwife, checked me again. "You are 4 centimeters."

I'm what? I thought. *How did I spend all this time and all this hard work to regress to four when I was five when I came in!?* Worst moment ever. I felt so disappointed and entirely lost faith in what I was doing.

Shortly after I asked for an epidural and as the words left my mouth I felt so disappointed. I remember saying "I want an epidural" and immediately thinking: *No, I don't want an epidural! I can do it without it.*

I kept saying I just needed some rest and sleep and Terry gently responded: "Nothing will make you sleep Paula, you are having a baby."

In the meantime, Mindy repeated, in a soft, reassuring way: "You are doing great... just stay with it." I felt so overwhelmed. I felt so sad asking for that epidural and could see my birth completely departing from what I had envisioned.

Alvaro's response was "let's wait a little more." A few minutes later Terry recommended starting some IV fluids just in case I was really going to go with the anesthesia. As the liquid began coming through my veins, I immediately felt so sick and scared, while feeling a weird, metallic taste in my mouth.

I freaked out wondering what they had put on my IV. I started throwing up while seating on the birth ball. I was bouncing on it and throwing up when suddenly I felt a huge pressure... My water broke!!!!!! This was sooo intense and felt so cool! I stopped making sounds and just stared at the floor. "My water broke, my water broke!" I yelled. I felt sooo excited again! *This is it. I'm close to the end. Forget any fucking drugs!*

I took my clothes off and kept moving and rocking. I felt reassured and went back to feeling strong and capable. I felt utterly overwhelmed but oh-so-empowered because it was true! I was close.

From that moment everything seems a little bit blurry in my memory. Certainly not as clear as everything I have just described. I'm not sure if I was checked again, but at this point, I got in bed and was on all fours for a while. I remember Mindy and my mom hugging me. It was so special.

I started squatting while holding on to the bar that hanged above the bed. Oh! That bar was amazing! I held onto it and felt so much pressure and remember being very loud. I yelled and screamed and felt a powerful urge to push. I guess it was time! I was pushing my baby down!!!!!! After doing this a few minutes, I laid down on my side.

Then I experienced the famous ring of fire. That was INTENSE! I felt as if I was yelling at the top of my lungs! Mindy grabbed my hand and placed it on my baby's head as she was crowning! That was the most unbelievable feeling in the world.

I pushed a little more and reached down with my two hands and grabbed my baby. I took her right up to my chest in pure ecstasy.

"Hi sweetie," I said, as I smelled and felt all the amniotic fluid and vernix on my baby. Few words can describe this moment. Very few. I kept my baby on my chest for a while before getting cleaned and dressed. I remember trying to get the baby to nurse right then and there, but she was as exhausted as I was. *Oh, my baby is here…my baby is here.*

Emma Nicolette Betancur was born on December 16th, 2009 at 12.58 pm. I will never forget this amazing day as we gently welcomed our baby into the world.

"The moment a child is born, the mother is also born. She never existed before. The woman existed, but the mother never. A mother is something absolutely new."

– OSHO

CHAPTER 8

A Mother is Born

The experience of her birth was a part of my daily life for many years. I thought about it daily during times of need. Times where my patience ran low, my energy low, and my trust low. Giving birth in the way that I did, empowered me to be a better mother and gave me the ability to believe in myself for a higher purpose than to survive.

The next three and a half years of my life were entirely focused on Emma. I read every parenting book I could get my hands on, took every holistic parenting/health class or online course I could. I went through so much information, seeking the ultimate best for this baby. I found a new side of me and created an entirely new identity for myself. The identity of a mother. I embraced being a witness to the beauty of providing my own child with everything I had needed.

Emma's birth, awoke more in me than I had ever experienced before. She helped me begin to see my inner wisdom and set me on the journey of searching for my essence.

My day-to-day focus was on parenting and taking care of her from my heart. But I wasn't always able to do just that. My desire to be an amazing mother was really consuming. My mind was constantly racing. My heart constantly dancing between feeling like the most powerful woman in the world and the biggest failure in the world.

I wasn't aware of it then, but this beautiful child was also showing me many wounds that needed to heal within me. I knew she came with that as part of her purpose, yet I felt so overwhelmed by the pressure of that role. For I knew what it was like to feel the pressure of taking care of a mother and I didn't want that for my daughter.

I nursed her endlessly for three years, and breastfeeding was the most incredibly bonding and connecting experience. I strived to take care of myself and my food as best as I was able. My husband was an amazing source of support. I will forever be grateful for the way he took care of us.

We had what seemed like a wonderful agreement. I would focus on the baby day and night, and he would provide for us and do some of the cooking. It worked so well. For the most part.

Until exhaustion set in. The amount of emotional, spiritual and physical work of taking care of young children is enormous. It cannot be put into words. It is not just the cleaning, the cooking, the feedings, the interruptions, tantrums, night feedings, and all the many other "duties" of the daily life of a mother. Yes, those are true. And they are incessant. But the biggest challenge of mothering? The biggest challenge has been to get to know me. To discover the deep layers of darkness within me that I didn't know I had. To recognize my weaknesses and strengths, my lightness and my shadows and merging all that into one. To confront them. Explore them. Accept them. Absorb them and love them. To let them go. Love them, because they present numerous opportunities to learn and teach and expand in confidence. And let them go, because they will naturally vanish when looked at closer, with curiosity and understanding without judging. This was the ultimate challenge and is the one that I believe will always continue to be a part of conscious parenting.

To do all of this deep work, while caring for a baby, and acknowledging that she too came here with her own agenda, her own inner calling and life purpose, her own healing to do and for whom I have been entrusted to care for and guide on earth, was not an easy task.

Nursing was the time when I could experience stillness, and it was the most wonderful gift. Perhaps that is why my own daughter insisted on nursing every moment of the day and the night.

At times though, the intensity of this work triggered an immense amount of insecurity and guilt when I wasn't living up to the standards I was reaching for. I was unconsciously consumed by a desire for more and more information but still didn't have a tight grasp on just being, on just connecting to my highest self. I realize now that I was putting so much of my power on external sources, techniques and information. My striving overall became so logical and so mind-centered.

I wanted every answer and perfect order. Luckily. I was surrounded by amazing mothers who were on a similar journey, and I'm so grateful because they shared that with me. They were often my connection with my heart space when I lost touch with it and got caught up in my head. I usually did the same for them, and it was such a wonderful and meaningful exchange of energy.

Our playdates were so much more than that. Every time my new mom friends - some of whom I met during my prenatal yoga classes, and breastfeeding support group - and I met to hang out, we connected in such deep ways. There was a power to our gatherings as we shared our purest most vulnerable spaces. Our interactions were full of empathy, uplifting words and encouragement to be the best version of ourselves. It was truly a meaningful and sacred space the one we could create by being together. We fulfilled in each other the thirst for intimacy women naturally have.

Mothering not only brought me a daughter as the most amazing gift but also brought me the gift of deep sisterhood; friends with which to share and navigate this journey and transformational time of our lives.

Because of this time of my life, I hope we are inspired….

* To feel empowered and proud of our accomplishments.
* To recognize that it is not what we do but how we do it that matters.
* To honor the insecure parts of us and love and accept ourselves.
* To let go of perfection but instead to seek authenticity from within ourselves.

*"Above all, practice being
loyal to your soul"*

– JOHN ROGER

CHAPTER 9

The Tools

There are many self-care tools and practices I began dipping my toes in as I finally committed to them as non-negotiable. I started experimenting and exploring their effect on me. These practices, such as Kundalini and Iyengar yoga, TMS meditation, aromatherapy, affirmations, EMF tapping, spiritual and self-help reading and many other conscious practices; little by little became a part of my daily world.

These tools and wisdom-filled practices helped me so much during the early years of mothering. They helped me cope with the day-to-day life, lifted me up and gently guided me when I spun out of control.

These tools and practices slowly became my way of connecting with myself. With God. Every time I took a few minutes to close my eyes or a moment to put a drop of essential oils on my chest, I chose to connect with my source, with my creator and in turn, he always filled me with love for myself and for my loved ones. For my baby.

As the months went by it became clearer to me that this motherhood journey had a huge purpose in my life and that it was revolutionary for my growth. It wasn't ever my focus to compare milestones or to achieve percentages in growth charts or purchase the newest electronic toy, but instead, my goal became to be the most loving and inspiring mom that I could be. To create a sacred environment of safety, love and nourishment for my child and her soul. Slowly and not always steady, my mothering became more and more heart-centered. My compass was Emma's birth, for the memories of that day kept me focused on the kind of mom I wanted to be, the one my child deserved.

Because of this time of my life, I hope we are inspired....

* To seek fulfillment within ourselves and not outside us.
* To find healthy ways to get control of our mind and our actions.
* To lead our lives from our heart and not only from our head.
* To allow our love for our children to be our motivation to be better every day.

"Perhaps they are not stars, but rather openings in heaven, where the love of our lost ones pours through and shines down upon us, to let us know they are happy"

– ESKIMO PROVERB

CHAPTER 10

Death Knocking on My Door Again

My little brother Santiago died on the night of December 28th, when Emma was one-year-old. His passing was shocking and unexpected. He was only 17, and took a part of me with him. A part of us.

A few days before his passing I had a terrifying dream. One that I knew had the same weight, as the visions and dreams I had of my dad's funeral, my baby's miscarriage, and my boyfriend's accident.

This dream involved a beautiful white ball of energy that was big and grand, with a gold shimmer and a vibrant rhythm as it turned and turned, but it was surrounded by five creatures that looked dark and gothic. They wore black and looked scary and evil. In the dream, I could feel the density and the negativity of the energy of these creatures and while it wasn't clear what this was about, I knew it was about something dark and challenging.

When Santiago died, during a drug-related robbery, we found out that there were five witnesses involved in his case. I was blown away when the Coral Springs detective mentioned this number, for it was the same number of the creatures I saw in my dream. Three of them were charged with first degree murder.

Santy and I were soul mates. He saw me as more than his older sister. He saw me as his confidant and his true friend. I saw him as my child, without the weight of the shadows our offspring reflect to us and with the hope, to also provide him with the support and opportunities I didn't have. I would do anything for this boy. His smile was intoxicating and his presence could never be ignored. We had a beautiful relationship and I had so many hopes and dreams for him.

After his death, I connected with him in an even deeper way. Right from the beginning I could see his smile and hear his voice everywhere.

The love of his soul was experienced by everyone who knew him. He had beautiful friends who adored him and we have gathered over and over during his birthdays and heaven-birthdays. We still do: listening to amazing stories and memories of him and of his goodness, kindness and gentle heart. When we gather, his friends and my family also often share about the many lessons we have learned due to his passing. His soul was so pure and so full of light.

Santiago was so loved and appreciated, and his death took me to a new place of surrender.

The stage of perfectionism I was in, the stage of external order, suddenly vanished. My heart again open and out of control because of the grief. The pain of grief hunting me again, a pain too familiar and well-known. It left me with no other choice but to surrender in humbleness and humility.

I couldn't go to that dark place of loss again. I knew that this time it had to be different. There had to be an acceptance on my part that was almost immediate. I had no choice but to trust that I could find the highest good in this new loss. I was no longer interested in figuring out why this happened to my family. I just needed to see that this was happening for something.

At the beginning, this something was about expanding my heart with more love and compassion than ever. For I was now a mother and could not afford to destroy all I had worked for. I could not afford to close my heart and drown in the darkness. I could only stay in the presence and the "beauty" of the sadness as it came in waves.

I chose to connect to Santy's transition from a higher place. A place of understanding that my brother was more than his body. That we are all more than our bodies. That we are all connected and united by the eternal life of our essence, our souls. I did that through my dreams and my prayers, my meditations and occasionally, by channeling messages through local intuitive and celestial readings by an angel practitioner and intuitive medium/channel, whose messages were always centered in a loving energy and provided me great encouragement, confirmation and connection.

I chose to live in the awareness that my brother surrounded me with his energy and purity of being. By knowing that his sadness and lack of sense of belonging had disappeared. He had been struggling with this for a while and a few days before his passing he called me to share his feelings. He was angry and heartbroken, feeling out of place in this world. "I wanna be with dad, Pau," was the last thing he said to me when we spoke.

I loved Santy like I had never loved anyone. My soul connection with him was so strong and pure. We could be with each other with the most ease and comfort. He trusted me, and I trusted him. I respected him and loved him unconditionally even when I disapproved of some of his doings.

I now understand that I was able to share this level of understanding toward his troubled teenage self because I too had lived the chaos of needing to escape my pain when I was that age. My pain was different than his, but his ways to cope were as harmful as mine. He just didn't get to stay on this plane long enough to realize and make sense of it here. Instead, his journey was back home, with source and with a higher perspective. Showing me, my family, his friends and my friends, lessons of pure gold.

I miss him dearly, yet I continue to be in awe for all the good he did for my life and all the pathways to light he keeps showing me.

Because of this time of my life, I hope we are inspired….

* To love unconditionally.
* To respect the free will of our loved ones.
* To experience pain without so much judgment and to allow it to transform us.

* To find all the things that make us like others and not otherwise.
* To recognize the impermanence of the body and the permanence of the soul.
* To help others who remind us of our own struggles.

"You were born in GRACE, let the world recognize you"

– YOGI BHAJAN

CHAPTER 11

Luna's Birth

My second daughter, Luna, was born on March 28th, 2013. A Thursday. Exactly the date I predicted she would be born. I woke up at our regular time, 6 a.m., and was feeling a little bit crampy. Emma and I made breakfast, and I picked up around the house while she played happily.

I was feeling like things were happening inside of me... but I was too busy to focus on them. We got ready to head to my midwife's office for my routine checkup. I decided to drop Emma off at Alvaro's office and head South by myself. She was happy to stay with papa. I made a quick stop before to get my eyebrows threaded and what a surprise it was to walk into the salon and listen to a Snatam's song! (She is a kundalini teacher and well known devotional, mantra, singer) *Ra ma da sa... sa say so hong...* (a mantra for healing with the universal energies of the sun, moon, earth as well as the healing energies within us) *This must be a sign,* I thought. *A great sign.* I was feeling great!

On my drive to the midwife's office, I kept noticing my belly tightening and casually glanced at the clock each time, to realize that the tightening was happening about every 12 or 15 minutes for just a few seconds… I didn't think much of it and kept driving. I got to Mary's office and had my regular visit. For some reason, I didn't really mention anything about these surges to her. I also picked up my birthing pool from her. I was so excited to set it up.

I headed back home and made a quick stop to get some lunch. Then went to the office to pick up Emma and went home. When we got home, around 3 p.m. I was really getting the hint that I needed some rest. So Emma and I climbed into bed.

Before laying down I pulled some angel cards asking if this was the day my baby was coming, and the response was as clear as it could be: "Yes! The timing is right for this new venture. A happy outcome follows your positive expectations" and a second card: "I am the angel of families; a happy change or addition is coming to your family." I got so excited! For a while I had been using these oracle cards to connect with heaven and with my angels and to seek answers and messages of confirmation and love. I slept while Emma watched a part of a movie. Then we got up and went outside to draw with some chalk and play *goloza* (hopscotch).

By this time, I was pretty sure labor had started. Playing *goloza* was quite a challenge, and I found myself staying in a squatting position as I bent down to draw on the driveway to get through a contraction before jumping again! *I'm not sure I have ever heard of a woman playing this game while on labor before.* At 5:30 I texted my sister saying I thought this was the day, and she arrived shortly after. Ahh! how happy I was to see her car. She was living with us at the time and there was no one Emma felt more comfortable with.

My contractions were strong enough for me to focus on them and only them. Alvaro got home shortly afterward and a few minutes later, my mucus plug came out. I called Mary to let her know and though part of me really knew this was labor, another side of me didn't want to believe it. She asked me to time the surges for the next 30 minutes. They were about a minute long and coming every five minutes or so. She told me she would like to come over to check me. It felt real then.

"I'm in labor," I told Mindy, my doula and friend to give her an update. She asked if she should come over now and I said we could wait until Mary arrived and checked me. I changed my outfit, got my comfy labor dress and my beautiful blessing way necklace on, and I did some laundry while Alvaro washed some dishes. I called Juan, my designated birth photographer and friend to give him an early update as I knew he could be far. I was so excited! I couldn't stop myself from crying in the laundry room imagining that pretty soon I would get to see my baby. *How is this happening? Just yesterday I found out I was pregnant again...*

Alvaro started setting up the pool. He was so nervous and was freaking out about the pump to inflate the pool not being there. Then I heard him saying the water heater was broken. Long story short, he sent my sister out with Emma to get a pump, and I was just trying to not get involved in the pool drama.

I went outside and sat on the birthing ball out by the deck and put on my labor dance music and started knitting. What a beautiful day it was! I felt so peaceful. Mary arrived shortly after and proceeded to check me. I was 6 cm dilated, 90% effaced.

I couldn't believe it. How was getting to six this easy? *Ahhh... gotta love being home*. I really believe that being home creates such a strong sense of safety that allows the mother to relax with more ease and thus open up. This was certainly my experience and while my first natural birth at the hospital was quite empowering and beautiful, nothing compares to the sacredness of birthing at home.

Mary, with her gentle smile and sweet voice, then said she wasn't going anywhere and started setting up her stuff. I texted Juan and Mindy around seven. "You can come over now. It's time" I said and they both texted back, "On my way."

I continued to knit away while staring at the beautiful clear blue sky. I could just stare at it forever. It was the bluest blue I had ever seen and the whitest little clouds too...I stayed here for a while by myself in pure gratitude and loved it.

Then Emma joined me and wanted to play. I kept squatting occasionally as I made my way into the house with her. We then had something to eat in the kitchen with Caro, my sister. We were making jokes and remembering all the monkey sounds during our trip to Lion Country Safari the day before. We were having so much fun and I was still finding it easy to navigate each contraction by keeping my eyes closed. This was when Juan arrived and so did Mandy, Mary's assistant. I was very excited to see Juan! I had been dreaming of these gorgeous pictures.

I visualized them on my walls and had spent so much of my pregnancy creating such a sacred space within my home and within myself for this birth. The experience of home-birth truly transformed my understanding of the home as a sacred space. A sacred space that most ancient ancestors recognized as a symbol of the body and womb of the original mother. A place where she housed, nourished, and protected us in her womb. This is how my home felt.

I finished eating and went into my room. The sun was going down and I started lighting up some candles. It took me a while to light them up as I often had to stop and squat through a bunch of surges that were getting stronger. I then went into Emma's room while Alvaro finished filling up the tub. I sat on her rug and meditated until a few minutes later I felt a warm hand on my shoulder…It was Mindy. What a relief.

My birth team is here! Complete! My pool is ready, my house is clean and beautifully decorated, my daughter is happy, and my husband is here. A huge accomplishment on its own since most of my pregnancy with Luna I worried that he couldn't be home since he was beginning to travel for work and to play racquetball nationwide.

I felt ready. It was a perfect day to give birth. Mindy and I chatted for a few minutes. We spoke about what a perfect day it was to be born and shared some tears of happiness. Moments that will never leave my heart.

Then I finally got in the water, and it felt amazing. My doula, Mindy rubbed my back, squeezed my hips, worked on my shoulders… We were happily chatting between contractions and I thought it was so cool because as soon as one contraction would come and my moaning started, everyone would stop talking and remained quiet during it. Then they would carry on with the conversation. Talk about respecting your space and feeling reverence for the process!

Emma kept coming in and out of the room. She brought me some artwork she made and a beautiful festive garland. She also came in with a basket filled with beautiful white rose petals to put in the water.

She fed me a couple of apple slices and finally wanted to come into the water with me. We hugged and played in the water and she swam so beautifully like a little mermaid while I closed my eyes to go within and ride it out. Each surge was a chance to transcend and each one left me feeling a little blurry and blissful as they ended. Emma stroked my face softly, and I felt so much joy with each stroke. It seemed so surreal that here I was, staring at my beautiful daughter, whom I gave birth to not too long ago; as she comforted me and loved me during the arrival of my second baby. These moments were just pure joy and genuine love. So magical.

The energy of love and wisdom Emma brought to my birth with her soft touch, her innocence and her deep eyes, allowed me to channel such a powerful divine presence through my body and my soul.

After a while I started feeling the surges spacing out a bit. I was beginning to feel so relaxed, that I decided I would get out of the water to walk around and move. Mary agreed it was a good idea, as I've been in the water for an hour and a half. Mindy suggested some lounges. I got out of the tub but didn't make it too far. I didn't even make it past the door of my bedroom.

Suddenly it all got hard, really hard and so quickly. I sat on the floor and all I could feel was Alvaro's and Emma's hands on me. My mom arrived at this time. They hugged me and kissed me so sweetly. This was the moment I felt truly overwhelmed and was the first time it all became pain. Real pain. Not intense, deep waves of energy and pressure as before, but pain. I cried hard and uncontrollably. Sobbing in a way that was so scary as well as relieving.

It was overwhelming, but somehow, I knew it was good for me. I knew this was "the gate of doubt". A "gate" I learned about through a Birthing from Within class and that refers to a moment during labor where the mom must find her way to move through a state of being and feeling of fear, or insecurity. It felt great to cry it all out! I really did know how to do this! Wow! No inhibitions, just letting it out. I felt completely immersed in my body and in the strength and warmth and fear that each contraction brought. My heart expanded, my body expanded. I could feel it. And amid the fear and desire to give up, I truly knew everything was fine. I was fine. Fully present with each moment.

Everyone came to sit on the floor and supported me. I was sitting in the middle of a circle, surrounded with so much love. Emma's hugs were filled with love. With power. So much strength in those tiny arms. As each contraction came, I claimed my space and bent forward.

I went back into the water after a while and what a huge difference the water made. I kept doing my thing, going within with the surges… transporting myself to other moments with the help of the music and the mantras playing in my bedroom. I smiled and chanted inside feeling the high vibration of such sacred sounds. Occasionally opening my eyes and gazing at all those beings near me, in my home and there for me and with me. ALL with me.

I wanted to absorb it all and I did. Beautiful sounds. Beautiful scents from Mindy's oils. Beautiful people. This is the joyful birth I envisioned and much more. This is my ultimate experience of genuine connection with the divinity of the true surrender of knowing it all by not knowing anything.

I started feeling lots of pressure and my moaning and grunting changed to a more intense tone. The pressure was more. There was no way to control it. It was intense and I felt so primal because my body was "pushing" by itself!

I kept my eyes closed the whole time and kept feeling the intense urge to push. I did. And then I floated. I floated in my back because there was not another way my body could stand being. I couldn't even hold myself floating, so Alvaro and my mom held my arms and I floated on my back. My body floated, and then my soul floated. I felt my soul leaving my body right then and there. My beloved brother was in my mind and at that exact moment, when I kept thinking I was leaving this plane and that I was dying (in the most beautiful way) The song "Go in Beauty," by Mirabai Ceiba started playing. The song we have played for Santy's celebrations of life since he passed. His song was up. And I was dying, on the same date of his heaven birthday, the 28th and at the same time of the night he died: 10:44. After I traveled only God knows where, a force within brought me back to my body. "Come on Luna, let's do this" a voice within repeated. We were paving the way from darkness to light and my baby and I were doing it together.

I pushed and I grunted and I yelled and yelled and screamed! I squeezed Alvaro's arm so hard and I could feel myself opening up. Holding my mom's hand for dear life. Alvaro got in the water as Luna's head emerged. *OH MY GOD*, I thought. And then, I could not look again or open my eyes even though I wanted to until she was out. I placed my hand on her head. Her soft hair was all I could feel. I will never forget that softness. I placed both hands on her head, pushed some more as hard as I could. Yelled with all my being and then… her little body emerged. Her hand up first! I opened my eyes and there she was.

WOW! What a miracle! She just came out of me! Out of ME! I reached to grab her and cuddled her in my arms in such awe! In such reverence. I held her on my chest and cried. Pure tears of joy. Of bliss. Luna Santy, whose first name comes from the Roman Goddess of the moon; her second name in honor of my beloved brother was here.

Emma came into the room right at that moment. The moment I had Luna in my arms. She got in the water and was speechless. Alvaro too. We stared at her. She was perfect. She was here. This was a dream come true.

"Instead of believing what you imagine, will something into existence, it is your openness to imagine a possibility that confirms what was already meant to be along the path of your current timeline."

– MATT KAHN

CHAPTER 12

Following the Call of My Intuition

I have spent much of my motherhood journey submerged and buried in books. I have read and read, sometimes fully absorbing every word and other times not comprehending or retaining one bit.

Shortly before the birth of my second daughter, Luna, I had a strong impulse to express my heart so fully. It was as if I could not put more information inside my brain and had reached my maximum of filling up with external knowledge. I was on overload and instead needed to take the time to embody the knowledge, explore it within, practice it, write about it, sing it and share it.

I started writing about my own experiences to validate them, to own them and to forget about overextending myself and running on empty to be of service to my family and putting myself last. I was being called to understand from this new height that my story truly had a purpose and that I was more than a survivor of loss and hardship. More than a caregiver and a responsible young woman and wife. I felt I was not only seeking for more, but deserved more, and this was not coming from an arrogant place or from a place of taking from others, but from a place of giving to myself the love and kindness I often extended to others. I needed validation and integration of myself before I could go on.

It was during my 10th year of marriage that a new phase of self-discovery arose. A phase where I was no longer in charge of "controlling" my journey but instead, continuing to co-create it as I followed the guidance towards a bigger purpose. I arrived at a place in my life, where being nice and put together was not the only option. But instead, I needed to be fully raw, real and authentic. I needed to honor others by knowing myself first. I needed to be motivated by love and not by fear. I really believe Luna's birth took me to this place of my truth. A place were masks could not be worn anymore and where the truth of who I was, needed to fully escape. I needed to grasp what really mattered to me. All the small and big details of who I am that matter.

This knowing came with a price off course. It was the beginning of shedding and of letting go. As I felt falling deeper and deeper into what I now call a breakthrough, which felt like a breakdown at times and included lots of tears, inner chaos, confusion, mood swings and an overall sense of unfulfillment, it started becoming very clear that my husband and I had shifted very far away from each other.

Even amid such turmoil, there was a sense of relief as I felt strongly guided towards a different path and as I began to feel love for my stories and my experiences and especially for my feelings as a starting point to create something new. I began to feel in love with my loss and my growth and entered a space of curiosity about myself. A space of beauty in the knowledge that there was a reason for all of my experiences and that lessons were waiting to be claimed from each and every single one of them before moving forward.

It was around this time that Wayne Dyer, author of many amazing books such as "Wishes Fulfilled" and "The Power of Intention," passed away, and I don't know why his passing was synchronized with such a shift within me. I had met him a few years back at an "I can do it" conference in Atlanta and I just fell in love with his teachings of divinity and gratitude and with his comforting presence. His energy was so present with me and it was so encouraging and beautiful.

I felt like he guided me towards a daily practice of expression through the written word. Sometimes in the middle of the night, I was called to just write with no formal order and without questioning what came out of me.

As I wrote, I felt I allowed my higher self and my spirit to dictate the words and I would just type. As I typed I observed the letters in my computer and they seemed different. They were calling me. They seemed full of light. Brighter and bigger. Just as I felt. Bigger and brighter even though it was not apparent yet.

Writing became a promise to me, to continue my self-exploration. To be curious about me, about the God-like qualities in me and my experiences and to declare my deep heartfelt intention to use this expression as a tool for growth and service.

I don't know how, but I knew that I was meant to be a source of inspiration for other women, mothers, daughters, sisters, and humans of the world. I felt that maybe I could make a little difference in other people's lives. I had many friends and relatives coming up to me to process their lives, or to seek a different perspective. This had happened to me since I was in school in Colombia. But at this point in my life, it felt so bizarre to give "advice" to others as I was yet to fully get a grasp of my own life. However, sometimes the words that would come out of my mouth would surprise me. Because I knew a lot of my advice or feedback to my friends was not coming from me, but instead through me. Regardless, I just knew these words and the energy they carried needed to come out. It was a calling. It wasn't my choice anymore.

Because of this time of my life, I hope we are inspired….

* To seek to the guidance within and not without.
* To stop seeking confirmation that our intuition is real.
* To be of service to others from a space of detaching from our limited self.
* To reach out to spiritual teachers and to be open to their presence when they show up.
* To have a sense of wonder for our own inner world.

"You can't run from the shadow,
but you can invite it to dance"

– TANYA GEISLER

CHAPTER 13

The Stirring & the Contrast

For the last ten years, I have had two different dreams with that amazing blue-eyed young man that I loved. One dream, every night of my life for ten years.

One of the dreams was almost like a memory. Us, fully present and lost in time in our romantic play. Our lovemaking. His eyes always my focal point. This dream felt so real, and my body reacted to it by turning, and wiggling and moving my hips while sleeping in my bed.

The other dream, not as pleasurable, was about him, showing up back into my life as if he was suddenly alive. I would be so confused and conflicted in this dream. He would show up to claim me as his and to ask for us to continue our life together. This was impossible in my mind as I was already married and had two kids. The dream ended with such confusing and painful energy and would leave me worried and sad.

Could I still be in love with someone who died over 10 years ago?

As I began paying attention to how long I had been having these same dreams, I also started feeling angry at my husband. Why didn't I feel that same level of connection with him? In retrospect, I was truly mad at myself and not at him. I was mad at myself for not trusting my intuition in recognizing these dreams as a roadmap for more fulfillment. But how could it be? Surely they were just memories. I continued ignoring these cues and feelings.

I began feeling consumed with unrecognized passive and steady anger. One that repeated my old patterns and habits of not acknowledging the feeling. I felt numbed. My interactions with my husband where limited. I was quick to be harsh and unkind. Passive aggressive. And he, not being interested in conflict, would just stay out of it.

As life got busier, with two kids, a house and my husband with more financial responsibilities and changes, I felt we were living separate inner lives. I was unable to express the sense of disconnection I felt. I tried my best, but I just wasn't doing a good job.

I felt like there was no way I was the same 19-year-old that got married in 2006 while he expected me to be. My soul had expanded a lot through everything I had experienced while being married. While becoming a mother. While embracing loss. While growing up.

With time, my anger could no longer be pushed down. I wish I could have explored my confusion sooner, before it became anger. Because it was pent-up sadness, grief and fears, masked as anger. I wish that I would have had the freedom to recognize anger at the time, not as something bad or negative but as a valid expression of the range of emotions we as humans experience. At this point, I suggested couples' therapy with a few practitioners, with no success. I was doing the best I could, but when the scarce chances to have this conversation with my husband came up, I was often unable to know where to start.

I felt grateful for what I had and what I had lived, he is such a generous and good hearted man, but I felt unsatisfied with the structure of my relationship. The absence of myself. The absence of joy and healing. The absence of connection. Soon Alvaro began to travel a lot more due to work. The physical absence did not help us. Mixed with the separation we had from the heart space, our lives were completely divided. Our kids united us and the memories of our life together too.

I entered a phase of such duality where I would have days full of a sense of gratitude and the next day I would have a huge sense of emptiness. I felt resentful and bitter and disappointed with my life and my marriage, and in turn then felt guilty and afraid for feeling that way. I had days where I felt I was living such a colorful and vibrant world inside that he couldn't see and that I didn't know how to share in a way he would understand or appreciate.

I felt I was struggling with the identity of a mother and of a wife and I felt so limited for being seen in that way by my husband. Being seen in that way by myself. I just couldn't put my finger on it and often felt so guilty even to feel that I was unfulfilled when my life looked so perfect. How dare I act so ungrateful? How dare I not support him instead of seeking to be supported? How dare I not just love him instead of attempting to be loved? But the cycle of anger, bitterness, guilt and shame danced around my days, and my months.

There was a fire within me that was burning for more purpose, and I wasn't fulfilling it. The bitterness was showing me that I needed to heal and let go of so much judgment. The disappointment was showing me I could not live in apathy. I had already done the work of tapping into the passionate part of my essence, of my core, of my purpose. I knew what I wanted; I knew what I didn't want. I just had to take a leap and do it, ask for it, claim it, live it, face it.

I felt consumed by the need to express this in a way that was understood or validated. Why did I need his validation and his approval so much? I felt like a child needing her parents.

I tried in different ways to communicate this as maturely as possible but I couldn't. I tried to communicate it more authentically and with more raw emotions, and it was not well received. I had a calling to live with integrity to myself and not with the standards of anyone else, but this was all so new to me. Or maybe so familiar to me. The feeling of being needed all the time by him and my children was making me feel exhausted. Depleted.

I craved to be seen as something more and to be welcomed with all my feelings and raging emotions. I wanted my partner to enter my world with wonder and empathy. Just like a child needed. I saw this in my children and I wanted to honor that for them, yet it made it more apparent for me that I lacked that. This was a big part of my healing.

I now understand the purpose of my dreams with Lucho. These dreams were signs and messages from my higher self and his spirit that pointed me to the direction of my heart. I finally recognized that the energy of those dreams was about aliveness, about passion for life, adventure, about kindness, about compassion, unconditional love and joy. These dreams were telling me that I didn't need to feel stuck in a place of comfort out of fear of the unknown or out of gratefulness for the past. I had outgrown my current life. I needed to feel inspired and to reconnect with the unique rhythm of my heart. To look forward to a future I had not yet planned.

Because of this time of my life, I hope we are inspired....

* To explore the meaning and guidance that comes from our dreams.
* To not ignore our anger but instead to use it as a catalyst for change.
* To seek only validation within ourselves.
* To be proud of being sensitive and vulnerable instead of ashamed or seen as weak.
* To take a leap of faith and embrace the risks of the unknown!

*"The parenting journey holds
the potential to be a spiritually
regenerative experience, for both parent
and child, where every moment is a
meeting of spirits, and both parent
and child appreciate that each dance
on a spiritual path, that's unique,
holding hands and yet alone."*

– DR. SHEFALI

CHAPTER 14

Mindful Mothering

From the moment I got married and talked about having kids, I knew I would be a stay-at-home mom. I mentioned before how having a miscarriage was proof to me that I wasn't ready to be a mother at that time. Losing that baby made me take the reins of my body and life. Refusing to go the in-vitro route, I stumbled upon the world of holistic lifestyle, conscious pregnancy, and attachment parenting. I am so grateful for coming across those doors that opened my mind and my heart to a completely new world.

As I embraced motherhood with these principles, I often felt lost as I strived to fulfill the labels of an attachment parent. At some point, labels come with strings attached: Judgement. And it is not just the judgment from others as they realize your life is not as perfect as it looks on Facebook, but it is self-judgment that becomes our biggest enemy. I have had my share of guilt trips. I have beaten myself up for not being kind enough, for being too strict, and because I could have done so much better. I have also had my share of moments where I have nearly collapsed and sobbed my eyes out on the bedroom floor out of pure exhaustion, fear and frustration while my sister held my hand.

It was during these moments that I craved and longed for my husband's emotional and spiritual support. His support was there in a very practical manner. His suggestions would often be to hire a babysitter or to have the housekeeper come more often. But for some reason this was not enough for me. My heart needed empathy, companionship, and a shoulder to cry on. I struggled with expressing these needs because I felt that what he offered me was more than what many other men offered. "I should be grateful instead" is what I thought, and what I heard.

As time has gone by, I have learned little by little to let go of perfection. I have learned to be kinder to myself, to be more flexible and always to look for balance. I have also learned more about what a woman's innate thirst for intimacy means and how important it is to fulfill that from within as well as amongst other feminine energies. I have learned about expressing my needs without being apologetic and truly validating how I feel first in all ranges and colors of emotions. The way we move forward in our evolution as men and women is with self-awareness and with a consistent commitment to be better, to learn and to share ourselves fully, in the most genuine expression.

After staying home for almost 9 years, and after facing many changes, I clearly can see that my parenting is more real and authentic now than it ever was. I relate to my kids with more balance and truthfulness because I have learned to relate to myself in that exact way. I realized I couldn't offer them the life I wanted to paint for them, without creating a blank canvas within myself first and without creatively painting my own world first. The choice of being a full time nurturer and primary caregiver, who selflessly gives herself in service to take care of the other when in need is what Yogi Bahjan called: Guru Dev. Meaning the teacher, the wise one who cannot be seen. The force of the unknown. The transparent guide.

All mothers know that embracing that Guru Dev isn't always easy. We often get caught up with our own agenda of what we need to do as well as get triggered by the screaming child who reminds us of our own childhood and our unanswered screams or requests to not cry. I know I have gone through those triggers more times than I can count. This is the work our children as teachers push us to do. To see ourselves reflected in them but to also trudge through that inner wounded child in us and work on ourselves without burdening them with our wounds. Instead, fully embracing them as their own entity, with their own journey and dealing with our stuff ourselves. I am so grateful for the journey of mothering I have been in. It has been such an incredible path.

I will never forget one morning in which I awoke so tired and so depressed. It was a morning after I had had one of those "big talks" with my husband the night before. As I remembered our conversation and went through it in my head, my eyes filled with tears and my body was paralyzed. All I could do at that moment, was come onto my hands and knees, in the middle of my kitchen floor and just sob loudly. I moaned as if I was giving birth, recognizing that those moments of birth were my rawest most instinctive moments. I had no choice but to surrender in this way and as I did, both my daughters showed up. Both standing one on each side, they quietly placed the palms of their hands on my back, and with complete acceptance, they held space for my pain.

It was one of the most wonderful and incredible moments I have experienced, though I initially struggled in my mind, resisting the fact that they were seeing me in this way. For a short moment, I wanted to just get up and pretend I was fine. But I just couldn't. Their love for me gave me permission to be real with my pain and my sadness. After this moment was over, I finally got up and thanked them for their love. I moved through my day as gracefully as I could and enjoyed their simple games and the beautiful forest stories they were sharing with me. My heart was full: of both fear and joy at the same time.

The focus of my parenting now, goes beyond fitting within the boxes of my own pre-determined standards of a dedicated, selfless holistic mom, and looks more like me paying attention to my own issues and my own tantrums instead of solely my children's. I continue to learn to be able to shift and to see each moment exactly as it is. When I forget and get triggered and distracted (which happens more often than not), I bring myself back to my presence as quickly as possible. Just like a mantra. Sometimes it takes long to return, sometimes not as much. But there is always a path to return to presence.

My changes and shifts have also helped me focus on mundane and ordinary activities like cleaning or cooking in a much more intentional way. It isn't always easy, as the mind offers many challenges to avoid focusing on the now by getting stuck in the past or worrying about what's next instead... but it is true for me that during those ordinary moments, there have been gifts that have been whispered to me. Accepting those simple and small moments as great gifts is a gift on its own. Some gifts come in the way of shiny hazel eyes, or the most genuine smiles and tears. Some gifts come in the way of dirty hands and feet and unruly hair. Some just come in the way of acceptance and of empathy and sometimes of scary reflections. The gifts of motherhood are endless and abundant and it is a choice to tap into them at every moment. Otherwise, they are very easy to miss.

As I moved onto a new chapter of my life, I was able to validate the woman I am and re-brand my identity. Not because I lost it due to becoming a mother; or because I no longer have the title of a wife, but because I have finally tapped into the essence of what I love to do, what I want to dream of, what I want to feel like, what I want to accomplish and how I want to serve. Instead of automatically going for opportunities that only allow me to stay afloat in a practical and logical way, I want to pick my path. Or rather I want to follow the path that is being revealed to me, with a higher purpose and a more mindful journey.

I have learned to respect my imperfection and to love it! And I have also learned to adapt to the ever-changing rhythm of our lives. I am convinced that my investment in providing my children with the foundation of being loved, heard, touched and respected doesn't have to come at the cost of my desires but instead, that the biggest gift I can ever give them is modeling a life fully lived.

As my mothering journey continues, I promise myself always to follow my heart as it guides me to treat my children in the way I wish to be treated and to treat myself in that same way. I am grateful for the broader perspective and understanding that my early years of mothering have given me, in recognizing that the world needs humans who are whole, thoughtful, loving and caring. And the best way to accomplish that for our present and future is by raising them that way.

Because of this time of my life, I hope we are inspired….

* To detox from judgment.
* To give to ourselves first what we want others to provide us with.
* To love being perfectly imperfect.
* To dream fully and with no reservations.
* To treat children as whole human beings and tap into the gifts they bring.
* To recognize that our children's souls have their own lessons to learn in this world.

*"We are all winging it darling,
that's what angels do."*

– HEATHER ASH AMARA

CHAPTER 15

It Takes a Village and a Creative Outlet

Besides the huge inner change within me and the more profound devotion to source due to the miracle of birth and mothering; friendship has been such an inspiring and meaningful gift of my journey. It has been key to my development as a mother.

The mothers and the people I have met during these years of birthing, baby wearing, breastfeeding, Kundalini yoga, and Waldorf education, have touched my heart and supported my growth in ways I can't do justice explaining. I am to this day still in awe at the depth of the conversations we can have in just a few minutes while we strap our kids into their car seats or drop them off at school. We can cry in a matter of microseconds and offer each other hugs that take you from feeling like a complete failure to trusting that you are a true goddess.

I have seen some of my friends give birth and go through tremendous health challenges. I have seen them loose and bury their children. I have seen them in the worst of their midlife crisis, having affairs, going through a divorce, changing careers, and coping with addictions. But more than anything, I have seen every single one of them grow and blossom into unbelievable human beings who never give up!

I have felt so supported by their love and their helping hands. My children see these friends as an extension of their family and feel safe in the presence of these amazing people I have been lucky to surround myself with. These friendships and community have kept me sane, offered me company, healed me when sick and helped me with taking care of my children in a way beyond physically doing so. I will always be grateful for these friendships and hold each one dear to my heart.

Allowing my creative energy to flow has also been a huge key to the continued sustainability of my identity. I think this has been key for me not completely losing myself. I believe that many women suffer from postpartum depression not only because of hormones and excess drugs used during childbirth but also because they are alone and isolated in their new world. They lack the support of other women who are in the exact same place or had gone through it before. They feel ashamed for spending their time doing things that feed their soul and feel obligated only to their children.

Some of the creative outlets I engaged in both during pregnancy and mothering were reading, writing, conscious cooking, yoga, drawing and crafting. And of course, designing rooms and sacred spaces and rituals. Any time I spent in any of these activities, I felt nourished and reenergized and empowered. I think new mothers need to be supported more in their solitude and in their connection time with themselves, for it is during these times that we can listen to our intuition and process our emotions and our thoughts and when we do so, we become better mothers.

I believe engaging in any creative activity is a spiritual practice, for creativity is the true seed of source. God himself is the creative source and force. When we tap into the engagement of being fully present with this universal language of imagination and creation of any art, whether dance, music, ritual or poetry, we allow room for the highest and biggest part of us to express.

Because of this time of my life, I hope we are inspired....

* To lift each other up and support other moms instead of competing with them.
* To seek support when needed without guilt or shame.
* To nourish our family with healthy food that is cooked mindfully.
* To tap into our creative child within and paint or dance away!

"*Each place is the right place, the place where I am now can be a sacred space*"

— RAVI RAVINDRA

CHAPTER 16

A Sacred Space, a New Birth

Many of the deepest, emotional and most traumatic and transformative moments of my life have taken place at home. During the times when my dear loved ones have passed, I have received the news while in my bed, sitting at the dining table or walking by the kitchen in my grandma's house. Times where I have been pregnant and my contractions began, I have labored on my bedroom floor, in my bathtub, meditated in my living room, knitted on my deck and birthed in my room. These moments have all been life-changing and deeply transformative. Also incredibly difficult and intense as you have already read. I know for sure that there is no better place than home to feel secure and safe during times of stress. To feel a sense of belonging.

When I heard the news of my young brother's death, my home gave me the peace to seek my angel messages and light a candle. Simple things which brought me comfort and support. My home, gave me the peaceful and quiet space I needed, to cry and express my deep sadness.

During the birth of my firstborn: Emma, which -as you know, was a drug- free, beautiful birth at the hospital, - all I kept thinking was how much I wanted to birth at home next time. I craved for the smell of my sheets, the sounds of my neighborhood, the dim lights I could control myself. I craved for the beautiful flowers I had recently arranged and my freshly decorated Christmas tree. I starved for homemade food and a cold drink!

The next time I was pregnant, there was no doubt. Home is where this birth would take place. And so it was. Surrounded by all my special people, my angel cards, my blanket, my candles, music and my Latin food. In my room, with the beautiful altar I created.

This experience truly transformed my understanding of the home as a sacred space. A sacred space that most ancient ancestors recognized as a symbol of the body and womb of the original mother. "This analogy of oneness with our mother's body formed the earliest spiritual beliefs. Before our own birth, we were indeed one with the mother- She housed, nourished, and protected us in her womb," - Laurine Morrison. As I embraced the breakthrough I was experiencing, which again; it often looked more like depression and resentment than growth, it became clear to me that just like during birth, I had arrived at the gate of doubt; that point where we feel incapable to keep going but that holds great power in our transformation. I used my home as a support system for me during this time. Creating a shelter of protection for my sadness and using it as my church.

Being in tune with these feelings of love and safety in my home and with my passion and skills for space planning, design and decoration, I conceived my new business; Sacred Interiors by Paula. This whole new project of fulfilling my purpose and focusing on my own life became a little bit more tangible.

With my focus for this birth - my business - I realized that our physical and material spaces are a reflection of our inner world. And when there's beauty inside of us, beauty manifests outside of us as well. Becoming a beacon of inspiration, a visual cue and a reminder for ourselves and others of the maximum capacity of light we can shine.

Sacred Interior's mission was created to design mindful and intentional living spaces that support my client's inner visions and are at the same time, functional, inspiring, and beautiful.

It is in our home where we can create the perfect space to practice self-care, to serve others, to practice tolerance and patience, to affirm ourselves and each other, connect to a higher power and nourish our bodies to carry us through. It is at home and with those closest to us that we can begin to change ourselves and in turn the world, for I really do believe peace begins at home.

Many of us recognize the phrase "we are souls having a human experience". I certainly do and I also recognize the challenge it is to be here on this Earth. It is not easy or effortless, and I have always found it imperative to surround myself with things that inspire me and spaces that make me feel good. As I have deepened my Kundalini Yoga practice, I also fully understand how important it is to have the right tools and environments that nurture our souls and strengthen our mental, physical and emotional capabilities, so we can in turn handle all the challenges that arise at every corner in this life with more grace, more radiance and more self-control.

My own home design, which has evolved and adhered to different developmental stages, lifestyles, and configurations of family members, has in many ways been my channel to create a clear idea of the life I have been striving to have and the person I have wished to be.

I have done this since my childhood, as I displayed all my crafts and my paintings around my room at my grandparent's house. Currently, my small new apartment is filled with symbols and visual reminders of my commitment to myself and to my family and to live a life of meaning and joy. To trust myself and my journey.

I believe our home should not be taken for granted and it should be treated with the love and respect of any Sacred Space. Home is the space where we live our day to-day life and where our deepest thoughts and our emotions are created. Where the most genuine parts of us come out to play and sometimes our darkest parts too. Home is a place for meaning, purpose and reverence.

And so, I tapped into the confidence I needed to fully accept that what I was so passionate about could become a career for me. Incorporating the foundations of my Kundalini yoga practice, my interior design skills, and my real life experience as a stay at home mom; I was now committed to make my design approach a spiritual one.

Sacred Interiors has now grown into a virtual program where I help women align their interior, the essence of who they really are with their exterior, making their home a Sacred Space. A space where they feel inspired to connect with their inner beautiful self and authentically lead their personal and family lives.

Because of this time of my life, I hope we are inspired....

* To set up a space in the home where meditation is a daily commitment.
* To surround ourselves with materials, colors and smells that nurture us and bring us peace and joy.
* To treat our belongings with respect and to teach our children the same.
* To be creative with the process of bringing beauty into our home.
* To share our gifts and passions with the world!

*"I don't believe in miracles,
I rely on them"*

– YOGI BHAJAN

CHAPTER 17

Birth and Death on the Same Day.

My sister Carolina and I had been very close for the last few years. Our relationship shifted from big sister to little sister rivalry during our childhood and teenage years, to collaborative sisters after I got married; to true blood sisters after I conceived Emma; to soul sisters after we lost our brother. She moved in with me for some time and during that period she got to share so much of my new mothering journey with me. She saw me at my best and she saw me at my worst.

She prepared to be at my home birth with Luna and bonded with Emma. There was no one I trusted more with my daughter than her and Alvaro. She knew Emma so well and put so much effort into learning my gentle ways of parenting. She saved me more than once from losing it with my daughter and often lent me a hand, so I could shower, nap, or cry in peace. She was also a huge part of my support team during Luna's homebirth along with my mom and my husband. She was there witnessing the miracle and the magic of birth and much more after that.

Shortly after Luna's birth, she moved out and unexpectedly got pregnant. Despite the surprise, she faced her challenge with such decisiveness and strength.

My nephew Benjamin was born exactly one year after Luna was born. Through her experience and by witnessing of my birthing and mothering journey, my sister also was inspired to have a home birth. She had the same amazing birth team I had and a wonderful disposition and understanding of the process.

She was courageously determined to be a single mother and entrepreneur and a conscious and holistic home birth advocate. Her home birth however was extremely difficult. It was long and painful and terrifying. I will save the details for her own book one day, because her story is incredible! But for now, I will focus on the impact this birth had on me.

First and foremost, I have never been more scared in my life. Period. The visuals and the energy of being there while she pushed for over 9 hours in pure agony and to imagine my nephew being stillborn crushed me.

I have never in my life prayed as much as I did that day or cried with more fear than I did that day. Miraculously, she pulled through and my beautiful nephew Benjamin was born healthy and whole.

When Benjamin was born, I had the amazing honor of nursing him in the first night. My sister needed her rest and he needed safety and comfort. She asked me to nurse him and I absolutely and without hesitation did it. I spent that first night of his life nursing him and my daughter Luna, while everyone else rested and in their dreams processed such experience. Benjamin is such an amazing boy! I could not express the love I have for him and I'm so honored for having been able to spend so much time taking care of him and bonding with him during the first months of his life. My sister's resilience amazes me. Her compassionate heart and her effort to forgive amazed me. I love Benjamin and the lessons he has come to teach us. Experiencing his birth, brought me to such a humble state as I recognized both the fragility and the strength of life.

Because of this time of my life, I hope we are inspired....

* To surrender to God's will and to trust his plans.
* To feel fear fully and without escaping it.
* To believe in miracles.

"Affection can withstand very severe storms of vigor, but not a long polar frost of indifference."

– WALTER SCOTT

CHAPTER 18

A Cold Path, Falling Apart

When I came back home after this life-altering experience, I was greeted by my husband. He greeted me with the normalcy of a regular day and with an annoyed tone of wondering why I had been away so long. My words could not do justice to what I had just endured. My old ways of lacking words for communication kicked in and I didn't say a word. Instead, I felt annoyed, exhausted and walked away.

I regret not having been transparent enough to share that day what I was feeling. There was no energy left in me. I wish that at that moment he could have felt my energy and just offered me a hug. I often replayed this day in my head. It was such a short and quick interaction that left me feeling so disconnected from him.

But this was the story of our relationship in that moment. There was minimal sharing of our mind or heart. Our interaction was practical and efficient. Our expectations, high and invisible. A recipe for disaster.

Over the next few weeks, my energy towards him was hostile and indifferent. Why wasn't he interested in bringing up the amazing news of a baby being born? In finding out how the birth was? How my sister was? I was blown away by this. I just could not fathom it.

As expected and due to my attitude, we were walking on eggshells and both became defensive. Creating even more distance between us. Our conversations became heavy, controversial and difficult. We were two broken adults, with stuck and pent-up emotions joined together under the spell of ego. I know he felt confused as to why I was acting so hostile, but I could not snap out of it. We continued to be disengaged and indifferent.

Over time and after the feeling of loneliness increased, I reached out once more to him and proposed to work on this marriage with the help of a third-party. Therapy, again. The topics covered in the couple of sessions we attended often ended up being shallow and lacked meaning. I felt invisible. Completely invisible. I knew my inner world was so full and so complex and my husband didn't seem interested in exploring it with me. I didn't seem interested in exploring his world with him. He felt unsupported by me. Invisible too. Unappreciated and unloved. Where did our love for each other go? Our dreams to be a family? It was all there, buried under the layers of fogged up pain.

As I try to reevaluate this time of my life, I often wonder if my capacity to express myself would have made a difference in our interaction. What if I could have been honest and shown my vulnerable, scared side sooner and just shared my experience of Benjamin's birth with no expectation of this interaction?

I prayed for my marriage with such despair. I played and experienced with trying to be more understanding instead of being understood as much. I toyed with the ideas and the concepts of being extra-kind and compassionate to him and being less absorbed in my new experiences and in my unmet needs. I yearned to be able to stop sabotaging the life I had with him. I yearned to be able to stop seeing all the flaws and to focus, instead, in all the good he had. I tried so hard to hide my weaknesses. I failed at this experiment over and over. How could I offer him what I wasn't yet fully offering myself? I was so conflicted. I had completely forgotten the feeling of connection to anything higher than me. I was belittling myself and stuck in duality. I was wasting his love for me.

I felt like I truly was a completely different woman and that he didn't know me. I hadn't yet fully known myself despite all the moments where I thought I did. My core values had changed, but I couldn't quite define them as I focused on all that was lacking in my life instead of all I wanted for my life. All the material things around me, the trips, the food, the wine, were not fulfilling anymore. I craved for more. I wanted to connect with him more deeply. With more presence and more vulnerability. More common interests and conversations that were more profound. Birth. Death. Longing. Those topics became my entire world and I often fantasized, remembered and wrote about these experiences.

Writing continued to be my refuge, and it was mostly all in the form of questions I posed to the universe. I was questioning every single feeling I had, and no answers came for a long time.

My parenting took a toll. My spiritual practice vanished. My patience was very low and my physical energy as well. I felt tired all the time no matter how much I slept. I often slept a ton and other times was up all night. I cried whenever I could and yelled whenever I could. I felt so alone in my own home. I was only fully able to show this side of me to some of those amazing women in my community. What would I have done without them? I don't know. I was able to fall apart over and over, and to trust that I would always have someone helping me get up.

I hated feeling so bitter but also could not stand shutting myself up and pretending all was well. It didn't look well anymore, and it didn't feel well either. I now understand this was a time of awakening for me. This was an important time of my spiritual evolution. How helpful would it be, if we had more knowledge ahead on what these difficult times in our lives are meant for?

The yogis recognized this time of a person's life precisely as that. A critical time of spiritual evolution. Samvega, which in Sanskrit means a sense of agitation or an intense disillusionment with life or the world as it is. It is a state of mind when one feels disenchanted with life and can no longer find meaning or happiness in the life they are living. This is, according to the yogis; a time of suffering that serves as a portal to self-realization.

The thoughts of divorce started coming through my head. I questioned them because I was afraid I was just going to attempt to escape myself while fleeing from a relationship. More guilt and fear invaded me as I struggled with hurting the kind and beautiful man I had married. What about my children? How could I do that to them?

How could I betray the long-term commitment I had made? I focused in taking all the blame.

Because of this time of my life, I hope we are inspired....

* To meet heart to heart with our loved ones and not let our fears lead.
* To see no lack within ourselves for we are abundant with love.
* To accept others perspective and to genuinely wonder and listen.
* To know we are loved.

"Even a stone and more easily a flower
or a bird, could show you the way back
to God, to the source, to yourself."

– ECKHART TOLLE

CHAPTER 19

The Desert and a Hummingbird

I could no longer take the despair and had to let go of the idea of fixing my marriage. It was exhausting to feel that pressure. After feeling so powerless and striving to manually change the state and the direction of our relationship with no success, I finally just took a step forward for myself and while still feeling quite shaky and afraid, I decided to take a trip on my own to Joshua Tree, California for a Kundalini yoga retreat/festival.

I desperately needed to reach for the tools of this technology that I knew worked. And I don't just mean I knew in my head but knew in my body and in my soul. I had let go of my Kundalini practice for a while and I desperately needed its comfort and the strength and vitality it offered me again.

This was my first trip alone since I got married. It was the first time Alvaro stayed with the kids for a few days on his own. He was ready. He had to be. I couldn't do this anymore. I needed space. Silence. Uninterrupted time. Not just a day. I needed a lot of time. I was gone for five days. I wished it had been more.

After I settled in my tent the first day I arrived in the middle of the beautiful desert, I cried and cried and wrote and wrote. Often stopping to take a brief nature walk so I wouldn't drown in the tears I was shedding. I spent the whole day doing this until the moon made its appearance and the stars filled the sky. I went for a walk and when I returned to my tent, this is what I wrote:

"I arrived on empty, with numbness in my eyes, numbness in my breath.

Sitting still, my heart expanded as if needing to breathe, remembering the sweet angel faces of her daughters.

The only reason this heart is alive is them.

I've arrived stirred up and restless. Busy. Rushed. Stiff. Sleep deprived. Exhausted. Afraid. Ashamed. Confused.

I felt lost and the floodgates opened with the memories of loss. Of separation. Of distance. Of not being wanted. Not being needed.

Not being needed... this echoed in my heart... not being needed. Needed because his heart couldn't beat without mine, not needed because I was the caregiver.

After the tears slow down, I'm out of the tent for fresh air. I see minuscule pink flowers of the desert that spoke briefly of hope to me.

Memories of words written by a longtime friend... "you are like the flower to me" the words of a muse. Of a teacher.

Then, faint pink and orange colors of a sunset reveal peace and calmness... a few steps more and the grand finale... or perhaps, merely the beginning: a hummingbird, fluttering joyfully, magically. So tiny, so tiny, so magnificent.

I stared at it with complete stillness and presence. My tears were no longer there. It was showing me something. The path of beauty. It showed up to guide me and propel me towards my true path. A reflection of my true self. I just knew it. A faint smile invaded my face. The first in a while. Soft warmth invaded my body.

I stayed here with it for a long time. Followed it as it flew further away and the moon shone brightly. Its energy spoke to me. I spoke to myself in its presence. I am on the right path. Even when the as is, is as it is."

I fell asleep after I wrote that. And when I woke up the next morning, I had a different feeling in my heart. I saw the future, still so unclear, but wondering, what if I, at the end of each day could somehow see beauty? Like last night's hummingbird and the flowers... Then I have hope... hope that one day I can see such beauty at the beginning of the day too and maybe even throughout the whole day. A hummingbird circling me... That was the pivotal moment that changed the course of my life.

Because of this time of my life, I hope we are inspired....

* To let nature silently speak to us and connect us to source.
* To recognize the miracles of life that are around us all the time.
* To take small steps towards joy when sadness has overshadowed us.
* To believe in and to allow love in whatever form it comes to fill your heart.

"Surrender to what is. Let go of what was. Have faith in what will be."

– SONIA RICOTTI

CHAPTER 20

A Craving for More Continues

As I experienced days and nights at SAT NAM fest full of contemplation, mantra, meditation and journaling, I was often met with overwhelming sensations of unconditional love from above. I slowly began to fill my heart with more. With spiritual practice.

I dived within with my restlessness and felt a deep desire to spend every minute of my breath in this space of spiritual connection and to be consumed in that realm of bliss and joy. This was not just an escape from the heaviness of my own world. Relief. The sight of light. A tool to cope. It was also a truthful encounter between the duality within me. This time within became the answer to my emptiness and the yearning of my heart. I wish my commitment and my daily discipline to this practice would have been more present in many previous times of my life. It sure would have made a huge difference and saved me a lot of time wasted feeling unhappy.

At times, fear crept in and made me wonder if the presence of this hummingbird was making me feel out of control as my deep wondering about my life escalated. I started to feel this hummingbird was a fantasy and I questioned if I was spending too much time daydreaming of a world that did not really exist. Was I really getting closer to spirit or being taken away from my own? I was glad I was alone in all of this. Not many would understand this crazy exchange. I was also deeply confused by feeling so alone.

I thought of it all the time. The colors of its body and the peaceful energy it emanated when it flew around me. I could not help but feel an immense sense of gratitude for the blessing and powerful gift of energy and for the vibrating exchange of such a subtle encounter. Whenever I wondered if I could reach for it through written words and spiritual presence, I would try it and every time I did I felt my soul lifting from my body, even without his physical presence. I named him Pablo.

Whenever I felt like I was crazy again for experiencing this love coming from a hummingbird, I wondered if I should stop connecting with it and deal with my reality more rationally. But then again, I was afraid this meant separating myself from a source of aliveness, joy and love. I decided I would continue to embrace this and fill myself with the sweet nectar it represented.

I realized that I could no longer expect to get this sweet nectar from a mere human being. That neither my marriage nor my children would ever fill me with this sense of love. I realized during this time that my DNA had shifted and that my cells were being filled with colors and movement. My heart was being held in a space of understanding, of emotional safety and love. The sweet nectar came from a much higher place.

As this journey within continued, I understood I needed to accept the parts of me that needed maturity. The parts that needed love and to focus on the development of my intuitive mind as my main source of light and guidance to fulfill my life purpose. I have had the signs around me all my life! Starting with my childhood. I could no longer ignore this. How crazy have I been with multiple decades of this intuitive language testing me over and over?

As my mind entered a place of silence within the sounds of nature, I connected with unlimited parts of myself. I was listening to the colorful call of my soul. I experienced in my body, heart, mind and soul what surrendering and trusting felt like. Pure freedom.

I returned home, feeling stronger and more centered. I had smiled! I had smiled. That alone was worth the trip. I knew my inner dance would continue for as long as it might, even with fear and darkness returning often, but somehow Pablo, reminded me that

I could continue to hold space for that fear and darkness because I was loved. Because I was worthy. Whole and powerful. Patient and strong. Because the universe had a plan, and I was committed to following it.

Because of this time of my life, I hope we are inspired....

* To smile at the feeling of love.
* To choose stillness as an active pursuit of our destiny.
* To fully trust our intuition for it is the language of the divine.
* To feel the love of God through unexpected exchanges.

*"She remembered who she was
and the game changed."*

– Lalah Deliah

CHAPTER 21

Falling in Love with Myself

I spent many days lying in bed and closing my eyes, feeling the energy of Pablo next to me. I felt him caressing and stroking my face. I imagined its sweet aroma and vibration surrounding me with so much love.

These experiences of feeling enveloped in warm love, eventually transformed into a time of self-care, deep relaxation and self-exploration.

As I entered that magical space of relationship with myself, I discovered so many possibilities. It was as if my outlook towards life had shifted. The colors of the sky and the ocean looked brighter. The eyes of my children looked bigger and shinier. The birds seemed like miracles of God. It felt as if this love from source was being poured onto me out of nowhere. Born like the small creek up in the mountains. This love became water in the desert, and light amid darkness.

I no longer questioned my dreams and my fantasies. I could actually experience them as if they were real in physical form. I knew that whatever my destiny was, whatever path I sought, this love would never leave my heart, this warmth would never leave my skin and the beauty of this heart would always be a source of inspiration and of life. There was no going back.

I began trusting that I was in my true path to beauty and wholeness. To authenticity and to freedom. To more healing and thriving. Not as a destination, but as a daily journey of discovery. I could feel the oneness. No longer separate from source. I was connected to this being that was across the country and that in itself, had to be proof that I was connected to more. I was connected to God. *God and me, me and God are one.* I felt transformed by the constant experience of feeling the sweet presence of Source within me. My yoga mat was my Sacred Home, no matter where I was.

Because of this time of my life, I hope we are inspired....

* To remember we are loved.
* To remember we are wonderfully made.
* To remember we are beautiful.
* To remember God lives within us.

"If you want to make progress on the path and ascent to the places you have longed for, the important thing is not to think much but to love much, and so do whatever best awakens you to love."

– St. Theresa of Avila

CHAPTER 22

Devotion

My time of writing became an act of pure devotion to this love of God. This love to God and from God. My prayers, which were more a conversation than a monologue, in written form; where dedicated to the joy and the ecstasy of feeling alive and unconditionally loved. They were poems to my beloved in gratitude as she filled my soul and my life. An offering from my heart.

> *"My love, my source:*
>
> *You center me in a way that I never experienced before. My fears and my worries settle down and fade when I connect with you in the stillness of my heart.*
> *Self-sabotage and doubt arise, but they don't stay for long anymore. They do not have an environment to thrive in this open heart you have shown me. They only come and go. But somehow, you always seem to stay.*

I often feel as if you are holding my hand and taking me to a grand gate of Transformation. Of joy. Of self-validation. Of surrender.
On the way there, you heal the pain and wounds of the past. Childlike innocence returns. Lightheartedness, playfulness returns. My guard goes down, and I feel so humble to experience this. I have learned to experience an open heart, and I'm finally looking forward to co-creating my story. I am looking forward to be a participant in writing the chapters of my life, and most importantly, of following the writings of my soul.

As I continue to visualize what this sacred story of mine feels and looks like I continue to watch the heaviness of the past and weight of the present burdens and embrace them with this union of the soul. I allow this to come and I do my best not to resist it, just like I learned in the amazing experience of giving birth. I continue to surrender and to enter that inner silence as I integrate and bathe in the beat of my heart. The beat of a heart that merges with all the other heartbeats around me. I love you Pablo. You have opened my eyes, my soul, my heart, my body. You have expanded me, and I am forever grateful.

Thank you for the colors you have allowed me to see. The colors of being a radiant woman. A radiant human being. Thank you for the profound realization that I am a complex being. That I am the essence of divinity, that I am worthy of thriving and of happiness and fulfillment. Thank you for showing me that I am capable of letting my baggage go and of shedding the attachments of who I am supposed to be. Thank you for allowing me to see myself in you and to experience you in me."

As I aligned with this higher sense of devotion and of faith, an overwhelming sense of responsibility to use this energy to serve came upon me. This is when the opportunity to become a Kundalini yoga teacher came up. The excitement and intuitive knowingness that this was the thing I was meant to do was incredible.

Imagine butterflies in your stomach but with that feeling, also a collection of visions of beauty and of purpose and fulfillment beyond what I could ever imagine for myself. Ego still somehow trying to convince me otherwise with fears and anxieties about it...But committed to follow my intuition, I did it. I signed up for the teacher training. I will never forget when I told Mindy my doula and friend who is also a Kundalini Yoga teacher. She very calmly yet firmly responded: "what took you so long."

Going through this teacher training was life changing. From the beginning of it, I was blessed to live as Joti Piara Kaur, the princess/lioness who is the sacred embodiment of God's divine love and light on earth.

Joti is one who is filled with light. Piara means one who is filled with love. All females in the Kundalini yoga tradition who seek a spiritual name, receive the name Kaur - the Princess/Lioness of God who walks with grace and strength throughout her life. Yogi Bhajan taught that every woman has the potential to attain this divine state and encouraged all to manifest it.

Becoming a teacher has helped me make even more sense of my family's experiences than I ever thought possible. I found new ways to heal and most importantly, found the gift of a new purpose: to serve others with valuable and practical tools that can help them deal with their life and fill it with hope, courage and self-respect, even when it seems impossible.

It is now my passion to share this technology with those needing it like I did; for the world really needs the presence of radiant, balanced, happy and self-controlled people.

"When saying goodbye hurts my heart, I know I am blessed. It is a reminder of how deeply I can love."

– LAURA LAVIGNE

CHAPTER 23

Closure

My marriage was a relationship that provided me with so much love, dreams realized, security and safety. We shared a life of enjoyment and abundance. We shared many lessons and teachings. We healed and loved each other when we both needed it most. We traveled, helped many and shared ourselves with many. We shared many meaningful moments. We were incredibly blessed.

I have learned so much about life with Alvaro. I learned to laugh when I had forgotten. I learned about sacrifice for another. I learned to pursue whatever I wanted and to not give up. I learned to use resources to help others in need. I learned to have a sense of humor and to not sweat the small things. I learned to dream and to enjoy seeing dreams become a reality. I learned about being accountable for our actions. I learned that I must seek wholeness not from a partner, but from within. I learned that sometimes to love someone is to let them go.

I see very clearly now that I spent this decade feeding, studying, and experimenting with my inner garden until the fruits of my labor needed to be harvested. He fed my soul without knowing it and gave me the space to grow. He also eventually, gave me the space to go.

He released me to be who I really am and I released him though our souls have clearly chosen to be a part of each other's life forever, with the bond of our children choosing us as their parents.

Alvaro is a beautiful man. His heart has shown me what it is like to be generous, compassionate, caring, disciplined and positive. He loved me deeply, as much as his heart allowed him and treasured me and my presence.

He showed me that there are shadows within us that need to be brought to light. They cannot be brought to the light by someone else. It must be our own courage that faces them and welcomes them, that accommodates them until they turn into light. I realize now that my time spent looking at his shadows and attempting to keep them at bay was not needed. Instead, it was my own shadows I needed to spend time looking at.

I strongly feel we were absolutely meant to be a part of each other's lives in this perfect way. I will forever honor him and love him for who he is, for he really showed me his open heart and its ability to love. And as I am able to take a step back and see him without the burden of expectation of a romantic relationship, I honor him even more. I could never have chosen a better father for my children and I'm so grateful we were able to experience together the highest type of love that a human being can experience, which is the love of our children and for our children.

We shared the sacredness of giving birth together and of being lost in laughter with the joy only children have. When I see him looking at our children, I see the brightest crystal-pure light in him. I would never be the mother I am now if it wasn't for his support and his love.

I feel our relationship has been good for the world.

We have inspired so many with our marriage, and we have served as an instrument of God to show even the most skeptical, that together we could lift each other up. We have healed so many wounds in each other. We have helped so many. We were a really good team.

One of the biggest lessons I have learned so far is that our soul makes contracts with other beings to learn specific lessons in this lifetime. I believe that once these lessons are learned, sometimes the relationship ends in order to move onto the next lesson needed. My lessons with Alvaro are not yet finished, for he and I have agreed in our souls to be a part of each other's life forever by conceiving children together.

As we make our way into a new way of relating to each other, I want him to know that I will always be his family. That he will always and forever hold a very special place in my heart, my home and my life.

My journey of healing continues and I am doing so without blaming him for things he did or did not do that made me unhappy. I will continue to process this relationship and to be accountable to myself of my shortcomings, and for the lessons I need to learn. I can only hope that his heart also heals and that instead of closing up, it expands even more. This is what heartbreak often does.

As we co-parent our daughters, they will always hear the stories of the amazing man he is. And I feel that once again, in a new way, we are able to serve as God's vehicles to inspire and show others that kindness and love can always win and that uncoupling and changing the way a relationship looks does not mean failure.

Because of this time of my life, I hope we are inspired....

* To forgive ourselves and others for their shortcomings.
* To be grateful for all relationships and experiences.
* To stand up for ourselves and speak our truths.
* To be accountable for our actions.
* To allow heartbreak to transform into love and compassion.
* To be aware that divorce can be done consciously too.

"I learned that courage was
not the absence of fear, but the
triumph over it. The brave man is
not he who does not feel afraid,
but he who conquers that fear."

– NELSON MANDELA

CHAPTER 24

Refurbishing the Soul

Ending my marriage has been the most courageous and difficult decision I have ever made in my life. I basically chose to jump off a cliff, for no particular reason other than an overwhelming calling from my soul.

I spent many months frozen in fear to take that leap. But it wasn't until I leaned into it and faced it with strength, that I was able to tune in to my heart seeking liberation. Not from a spouse but from limiting mindsets and beliefs I was living with. My soul was seeking to fulfill its destiny full of greatness and joy and peace and happiness and I had to take that leap into the unknown to embrace my calling. To feel alive. And to find refuge in the solitude of myself.

So many of the broken pieces within me continue to come together and I am learning more and more every day to live in the willingness to expand and to be open to the flow of the universe. I am learning to live each moment as it comes, and without such a strict and set plan on how each moment should look and be like.

My heart continues to be refurbished, my soul reborn and I have a deep sense of gratitude for each moment no matter how challenging it might seem. Facing the fear of divorce has shown me the way back to myself. I was running on empty because I was placing everything and everyone on the seat of my identity.

This new transition is a new opportunity to re-design my life. A new chance to fully listen to the deep voice of my intuition and follow its divine guidance even when nothing much makes sense to the human mind. This opportunity has become a chance for me to engage in the unexplored parts of my dreams with humility and courage. It is a new opportunity to create vows to myself and to appreciate the beautiful life I have created so far, honor it and move forward.

I have learned to pray for my highest good and to trust in the spiritual guidance of what that journey looks like. I stopped praying for a specific outcome because I have realized how diminishing that is for the infinite power of the creator.

I am choosing to live my day to day in a new space of connectedness with myself and with the world. I am now enjoying the small moments of life more than I ever did. I do not want to miss those colors, because like the hummingbird showed me: they are vibrant and radiant! I am choosing to play the game of living in attunement to myself and just following and trusting the process as scared and as resistant as I might be. I am choosing to connect to my heartbeat and to my breath and to do so in gratitude for the opportunity to be on this earth.

By aligning my interior, the essence of who I am, with my exterior; I was able to solve the overall sense of un-fulfillment, lack of connection, stressed out and overworked feelings I was often struggling with and I'm honored to be a support to others to achieve the same.

Because of this time of my life, I hope we are inspired....

* To have the courage to make sacrifices for a bigger picture to take place.
* To tune into our heartbeat and our breath.
* To explore our dreams and design our life.
* To trust in the abundance of the universe.

"Baby, don't you know? That you have the entire universe waiting for you to discover it?

- ANONYMOUS

CHAPTER 25

Magic and Happiness – A Commitment to Myself

As I settle into my new beginning and experience the capacity to fully open the heart and allow it to feel a wide range of emotions, without them necessarily leading my way, I feel in awe of all I have learned. I am 32 years old, and my life has been full. I am in awe of the power of spirits' guidance and the ability to manifest and create the intentions of the soul. I bow down in reverence to the creator, to the teachers I have met along the way and to the teacher within myself. My wish for you is to be able to experience that too.

All these times of my life, have inspired me to heal further than I ever imagined. As I finish this book, I am inundated with melancholy from many of these memories. I also still vibrate from the memories of love and of joy. I recognize this book and these stories of my life continue to be digested and absorbed. But more than anything all these past times of my life have allowed me to be able to move forward into the new chapters of my life, with complete trust in the power of light winning over darkness. I recognize the dance of hibernating in the dark caves of pain and feeling and flying in the shiny and blissful, miraculous joy of love and connection.

I am grateful to know how to tune into the portal of loving energy and to connect to the chain of golden wisdom that surrounds us at all times, and that allows us to be effortlessly pulled into its striking beauty. I promise to myself to embrace the lessons of complete surrender as I stay committed to the intentions of my heart. My wish for you is to be able to experience that too.

I promise to myself to trust in my capacity to be curious and thirsty for life as I explore the adventures of the world with lightheartedness and ease. My wish for you is to be able to experience that too.

I have never been so excited to be alive, to claim my visions and my dreams and I'm finally ready to channel the courage I have learned to have, in a way that is more purposeful than mere survival. I'm ready to channel my courage to do what I am meant to be doing and to be the messenger I am supposed to be. I am ready to claim the gifts of the hardship I have endured and the pain I have felt. I am lucky to be surrounded by so many inspiring people who have again and again shown me their ability to live, to love and to thrive! I am ready to experience and witness the ripple effects of choosing a life of light and of creative potential. I am ready to follow the path of beauty in full communication with my beloved creator. My wish for you is to be able to experience that too.

SAT NAM!

CLOSING MANTRA

Mool mantra - A mantra to remove fate and our destiny to complete prosperity

Mul Mantra, the words first spoke by the spiritual master Guru Nanak after enlightment, literally translates as the "Root Mantra", or the mantra from which all other mantras in the Kundalini Yoga tradition are built.

Its vibration holds such power that it can transform your fate and help you rewrite your destiny with the ever-present love and grace of God.

Please visit 3ho.org for more info.

Mantra:

Ek Ong Kar, Sat Nam, Karta Purkh, Nirbao Nirvair, Akal Moorat, Ajoone, Saibhung Gur Prasad, Jap. Add such, Jugaad Such, Hai Bhee Such, Nanak Hosee Bhee Such.

Translation:

*"One spirit beyond, moves within the Creation –
Coordinating, consolidating, continually creating.
And this spirit within me, is my true identity.*

It does all and causes all to be done.
It protects me through all incidents of time and space.
It fears nothing and knows nothing of vengeance or anger.
Deathless it comes into form.
In itself, it has never been born.
Flowing through cycles
Of birth and death,
It moves by its own
Purity and projection.
This understanding
Shall come to you as a sweet blessing.
As a gift.
In every moment
Continue
In its continual remembrance.
From the start
This truth was true.
All through time
And space
Is true.
Even now
This truth is true.
Ever shall be true."

ACKNOWLEDGMENTS
AND GRATITUDE

I am grateful for my dad Joaquin and my mom Dora for giving me life. I am grateful for my mom and the teachings she has unknowingly given me.

I am grateful for the love and support of my brother, Santiago and my sister, Carolina, who are my biggest supporters both in earth and heaven.

I am grateful for my children, Emma and Luna who have awoken me at the speed of light! May you know that I do not strive to be your perfect mother but rather to be as real and as aware as I can of myself so that I may continuously release you to live your own truthful journey on this earth. You are my greatest teachers!

I am grateful for Alvaro, the father of my children, for all the love, joy, support and lessons of life he has shown me.

I am grateful for Rolf Johnson, who always encouraged me to dream big, to be happy and who always believed in me. Anthony Benitez, my dear brother's friend, who through sharing his own story with me and with many, has opened my heart to see beyond the masks of our wrongdoings, to see right through the goodness of our hearts and who is the embodiment of resilience.

I am grateful for the inspiring women and soul sisters that have accompanied me in this crazy journey of life: Veronica Ferrer, Aida Castro, Mindy Galamaga, Mara Lalonde, Kristen Kapur, Lea Leite, Jaime Valls, Davina Ferreira, Yeletsy Garzon, Cheryl Bougie, Anaie Amorim, Stacy Scheile, Deb Mele, Teri Brick, and many, many more women from my Kundalini and Waldorf community that I couldn't possibly attempt to mention. Thank you for your energy, your light, and your prayers!

I am grateful to Luis, for his beauty, his love and his spirit.

I am grateful for Pablo who inspired a new direction of beauty in my life, and who guided me to seek the nectar within myself.

GIVING BACK

Y.O.G.A For Youth

Proceeds from books sold as well as from Sacred Interiors Academy, benefit Y.O.G.A For Youth.

The Y.O.G.A. for Youth mission is to provide urban youth with tools of self discovery that foster hope, discipline and respect for self, others and community. The organization is dedicated to creating opportunities for urban youth to practice yoga and relaxation in schools, community facilities, hospitals and detention centers. http://www.yogaforyouth.org/south-florida/

Sacred interiors academy
Helping women align their interiors, (the essence of who they really are) with their exteriors, making their home a Sacred Space, so that they are able to confidently and authentically lead their personal and family lives, bringing more BEAUTY, LIGHT and PEACE to their world. http://www.sacredinteriorsacademy.com/

INSPIRATIONAL READING

Below are some of my favorite books. Books that have inspired my journey. Enjoy!

* A Return to Love – Marianne Williamson
* The Daily Love – Mastin Kipp
* Finding my ALEGRIA - Davina Ferreira
* The Conscious Parent – Dr. Shefali Tsabary
* Conscious Uncoupling – Katherine Woodward
* Kundalini Yoga – The Flow of Eternal Power – Shakti Parwha Kaur Khalsa
* The Power of Now – Eckhart Tolle
* Birth Breath Death – Amy Wright Glenn
* Love Always Petra – Jane Scovell & Petra Nemcova
* Soul Shaping – Jeff Brown
* Braving the Wilderness – Brene Brown
* Claim your power – Mastin Kipp

Printed in the United States
By Bookmasters